PREPARE

J. PAUL NYQUIST

FOREWORD BY DR. DAVID JEREMIAH

LIVING YOUR FAITH IN AN INCREASINGLY HOSTILE CULTURE

MOODY PUBLISHERS

CHICAGO

Edited by Elizabeth Cody Newenhuyse
Interior design: Ragont Design
Cover design: Studio Gearbox

ISBN: 978-0-8024-1256-0

We hope you enjoy this book from Moody Publishers. Our goal is to provide high-quality, thought-provoking books and products that connect truth to your real needs and challenges. For more information on other books and products written and produced from a biblical perspective, go to www.moodypublishers.com or write to:

Moody Publishers
820 N. LaSalle Boulevard
Chicago, IL 60610

1 3 5 7 9 10 8 6 4 2

Printed in the United States of America

This book is realistic, clear, biblical, and challenging. I earnestly believe that this
is the book for us in this generation as we face an increasingly hostile culture that
seeks to silence the Christian voice. Dr. Nyquist helps us face our foreboding
future with optimism, reminding us that biblically and historically the church
has always been the object of persecution by the world. I heartily recommend this
book to all within the body of Christ who feel a sense of despair over the fate of
our nation and the increasing attacks on religious liberty. We urgently need to
Prepare for the days ahead. This book shows us the way.

DR. ERWIN W. LUTZER
The Moody Church, Chicago

Luther once remarked that we should not be startled by persecution but strengthened by it. We must always remember that the Christian church was birthed in
the context of persecution and that the Scriptures themselves teach that believers
in Christ will be persecuted. In fact, the theme of suffering is interwoven in every
book and text. A theology of persecution is enormously important for believers in
the Lord Jesus if they are to walk faithfully in obedience to Him. I am thankful
Paul Nyquist is addressing this topic—a topic that demands careful biblical and
theological reflection.

DR. ALBERT MOHLER
President, The Southern Baptist Theological Seminary

In just a few short years, our culture's view on Christian principles and biblical
morality has shifted from indifference and skepticism to outright opposition and
hostility. Paul Nyquist offers a practical, hope-filled primer to help believers persevere and shine the light of Christ in the darkness.

JIM DALY
President, Focus on the Family

The question of persecution of Christians in America is not if but *when*—and most
believers in this country are not ready. Dr. Nyquist offers a biblical wakeup call on
how to respond with both truth and compassion. His urgent message is clear: the
time to prepare for the howling winds of persecution is *now*.

JANET PARSHALL
Radio Host, *In the Market with Janet Parshall*

As Christian persecution grows in the United States, Christ's people must be
prepared to shine His light into the darkness of hatred and spiritual warfare.
Dr. J. Paul Nyquist gives urgent, biblical insight for Christians living in a hostile
culture. *Prepare* is a must-read for Christian leaders and thinkers.

JOHN S. DICKERSON
Author of *The Great Evangelical Recession*

This is a terrifying, edifying, hopeful, and practical book for all followers of Christ.
Just read the introduction and you'll know why.

PATRICK LENCIONI
New York Times bestselling author

There are parts of the Bible skipped over by many of us who regularly read the Word of God—including the topics of suffering and persecution. Dr. Paul Nyquist leads us to those hard parts and helps us hear what God has to say.

Dr. Leith Anderson
President, National Association of Evangelicals

A must-read book for every citizen! Dr. Nyquist masterfully outlines the problems in our nation, biblically explains the principles, and eloquently lays out the plan that future generations are counting on us to accomplish. Dr. Nyquist implores the church to take the right stand, the right way, and with a right spirit. This book is the biblically balanced response to the tidal wave of change sweeping our nation. We all need to be prepared!

David C. Gibbs III
President and General Counsel of the National Center for Life and Liberty
Host of Moody Radio's *Law Talk Live*

Paul Nyquist is truly a "Son of Issachar" for the church today—a man raised up by God who understands the times, and through his outstanding book *Prepare* has given us knowledge as to what we are to do! *Prepare* is a must-read! A book for now—profound, practical, and truly preparatory for the difficult days ahead. I am recommending it everywhere I speak. Every believer ought to study this book!

Kay Arthur
Cofounder of Precept Ministries Int'l., Author and Speaker

As the powerful winds of cultural change blow across our country, God's people need to be anchored firmly to God's Word. *Prepare* provides the biblical principles and encouragement we need to live righteous lives in unrighteous times.

Josh D. McDowell
Author and Speaker

The great church father Tertullian once said, "The blood of the martyrs is the seed of the church." The same is no less true today. Whether persecution costs believers their livelihoods or their very lives, Dr. Nyquist has provided something very important for God's people in his warning, encouragement, and sage advice.

Dr. Glenn T. Stanton
Director of Family Formation Studies at Focus on the Family
Author of *The Family Project* and *Loving My (LGBT) Neighbor*

Dr. Paul Nyquist gives a clarion call reminding us that more persecution is coming and exhorts Christians to respond with compassion, not anger. Nyquist's message is important for anyone who desires to make an impact for the gospel in this twenty-first century.

Dr. Christopher Yuan
Author and Speaker

To the persecuted church around the world
Your example inspires us
Your encouragement humbles us
To God be the glory!

130485

CONTENTS

FOREWORD

Wherever I go these days, I seem to be confronted with one question: "Do you think God is finished with America?" I usually answer that question like this: I don't believe God is finished with America, but I fear that America may be finished with God!

For all of our efforts to preserve the soul of our nation, we are failing. We are losing the spiritual war and we have already lost the cultural war. Citing leaders John S. Dickerson, Erwin Lutzer, and Billy Graham, Dr. Paul Nyquist warns that we have crossed an invisible line, the die is cast, the tipping point has been reached, and apart from a gracious intervention from God, this nation is not going back to the culture and values it held in the past.

In other words, *Roe v. Wade* will never be overturned. The sanctity of marriage is a relic of the past, and God will never again be welcome in our schools.

How did this happen? In the first section of *Prepare*, Dr. Nyquist cites a five-step process that details the abandonment of our values and then lists the major court decisions that have pushed us along that way. These decisions resulted in the removal of the Bible from public schools (1962); the right to kill our unborn (1973); the removal of the Ten Commandments from public display in our schools (1980); the rescinding of the requirement for minors to gain parental consent for an abortion (1992); the provision for homosexuals to gain protected status as a minority group (1996); and the legality of gay marriage (2003).

I have read many books about the declining culture of America but none that so clearly explains where we are and how we got here. In the second section, Dr. Nyquist helps us to understand what this massive cultural shift means to us as followers of Christ. Because we stand apart from the world as it has become, because we are different, because we bear Christ's name, and because we expose the world's sin, we have become a hated people.

For two centuries, American followers of Christ have been protected from persecution, but those days are over. As we move forward into the next decade, suffering will become the new normal for believers!

How then are Christians to live their faith in this new, increasingly hostile culture? Dr. Nyquist challenges us to accept suffering as our lot. He reminds us that "all who desire to live a godly life in Christ Jesus will suffer persecution" (2 Timothy 3:12). The issue is not whether we will suffer, but how we will handle it when it comes. The extended section on the value and blessing of suffering is worth the price of the book alone! I predict that someday in the not-too-distant future, you will be trying to find these words again.

Chapter 9 chronicles many stories from the persecuted church. Read these stories carefully. They are a picture of where we are headed unless God intervenes.

The last section of the book is what I would call the "Hope Section." Here we are encouraged to choose optimism over pessimism. All three persons of the Trinity are available to us in our time of suffering and tribulation. Our Father is the "God of hope" (Romans 15:13). Our Savior is "Christ in you, the hope of glory" (Colossians 1:27). And the Holy Spirit is our "Helper" or "encourager" (John 14:26).

While our ultimate hope is in the return of Christ to take His people home, our immediate hope is in the return of Christ to bring revival to His church. I believe this is our only hope as a nation. Dr. Nyquist offers a compelling look at the history of revival in our land—and provides hope for the future.

I am asked to write forewords and endorsements for many books.

I have always made it my policy never to write an endorsement or foreword for any book that I have not fully read. As I read this book, I was thankful for that policy. I needed to read every word. I needed to understand every concept. I believe that God sent this book to me for such a time as this. I hope you, too, will read every word and look up every Scripture. Let the truth of this powerful message wash over your heart.

DR. DAVID JEREMIAH

INTRODUCTION

To be right with God has often
meant to be in trouble with men.

A.W. TOZER

In October of 2014, five Houston area pastors were ordered by the city government to turn over any sermons, emails, and text messages dealing with homosexuality, gender issues, or Houston mayor Annise Parker. The city's subpoena came as opposition mobilized against Houston's new nondiscrimination ordinance, Houston Equal Rights Ordinance (H.E.R.O.), which, among other things, allowed men and women to interchangeably use restrooms. A petition drive gained nearly three times the necessary signatures to place a referendum on the ballot. When the city threw out the petitions, a lawsuit resulted.

The five pastors were not parties to the lawsuit. While deeply opposed to the morality of the new ordinance, they had not taken any legal action. They had merely encouraged their church members to sign the petitions. Yet the city powerfully moved in an effort to silence their voices. It demanded they turn over all communications. If they refused to comply with the subpoena, they were threatened with contempt of court and jail.[1]

This would be a shocking development in any state of our union. In Texas, which sits squarely in the buckle of the Bible belt, this is nearly incomprehensible.

Mayor Parker later rescinded the subpoenas after the city's actions sparked negative reaction nationwide. But the controversy demonstrates what we're in for as believers.

Get ready. An exciting, yet terrifying era is beginning for American believers. As cultural changes sweep our country, we'll soon be challenged to live out what the Bible says about confronting and responding to persecution.

For nearly 250 years, Christians in America were able to live in relative freedom from persecution. We escaped because our society historically embraced and promoted biblical values. Our founding fathers penned a Constitution esteeming religious freedom and establishing that rights come from God, not the government.

Foreign leaders have recognized America's uniqueness ever since the early years of our nation.[2] While this can be a blessing, the freedom we have enjoyed makes us an outlier among the nations. Believers in much of the world regularly encounter persecution, prosecution, and even execution. The World Evangelical Fellowship estimates two hundred million Christians live under a daily threat of imprisonment or torture; twice as many reside where laws discriminate against them.[3] Persecution is the global norm. Americans are the anomaly.

But we're witnessing an epic change in our culture—a spiritual climate shift threatening to reshape life as we know it. Hostility and intolerance are replacing toleration. Rejection and even hatred are pushing aside acceptance.

> **PERSECUTION is the global norm. Americans are the anomaly.**

John S. Dickerson, in his well-researched book *The Great Evangelical Recession*, writes, "In the coming decades United States evangelicals will be tested as never before, by the ripping and tearing of external cultural change—a force more violent than many of us expect. Evangelicalism in the United States has stood strong through centuries of difficulties and setbacks. She has not seen anything quite like what she will see in the next fifty years."[4]

What's coming? Dickerson makes four observations:

1. The United States' broader host culture is changing faster than most of us realize.
2. The change includes pro-homosexuality and anti-Christian reaction.
3. The rate of the change will accelerate as the oldest two generations die, taking their traditional values and votes with them.
4. These changes will reach an intensity where they directly affect the church and our lives as individual evangelicals.[5]

Dickerson isn't alone in his prophetic storm warnings. Other highly respected Christian leaders are sounding the alarm. Dr. Erwin Lutzer, longtime pastor of the historic Moody Church, writes,

> We have crossed an invisible line and there are no signs that we are capable of turning back. Like a boat caught in the mighty torrent of the Niagara River, we are being swept along with powerful cultural currents that just might put us over the brink. Seemingly irrevocable trends put in motion forty years ago continue to gather greater momentum and speed. Our Judeo-Christian heritage that gave us the freedoms we have enjoyed is for the most part gone, and in its place is an intolerant form of humanism that can boast of one victory after another. The "cultural war" we used to speak about appears to be over, and we have lost.[6]

Even Billy Graham, as he reflects on more than ninety years of life, notes today's troubling state of affairs. "Our society is caught up in a powerful windstorm that has already caused massive destruction, with the full impact yet to come. . . . Now, at ninety-one years of age, I believe the storm clouds are darker than they have ever been. The world has dramatically changed."[7]

We all hear these warnings, but I know for many of us it's hard to connect the dots between our rapidly changing culture and persecution the way we normally think of it. We may realize society has changed, and we may discern shifting values, but perhaps we have not personally experienced hostility from our culture—yet. So we may wonder if this will affect our lives. But persecution wears many faces—as we'll see.

WHAT DOES IT MEAN TO BE "PERSECUTED"?

Let's define our terms. Because of our relative inexperience, we Americans tend to have a limited view of persecution. We typically think of it in physical terms (imprisonment, martyrdom), and as such, may question whether our experience truly qualifies as persecution. But this definition is too narrow. The biblical term suggests a broader view including aggression, oppression, and violence affecting the body, mind, and emotions.

Theologian Geoffrey Bromiley's definition is one of the best: "Persecution is the suffering or pressure, mental, moral, or physical which authorities, individuals, or crowds inflict on others, especially for opinions or beliefs, with a view to their subjection by recantation, silencing, or, as a last resort, execution."[8]

Simply put, *persecution is the societal marginalization of believers with a view to eliminating their voice and influence.* Its tactics can span a wide spectrum depending upon the severity of measures needed to eradicate the voice of a follower of Christ. *Christianity Today* stated, "While martyrdoms did double in 2013 (to more than 2100 deaths), most persecution is not violence. Instead, it's a 'squeeze' of Christians in five spheres of life: private, family, community, national, and church."[9]

Therefore, when we think of impending persecution, we need not think of death marches or churches burned. While some physical retribution could eventually emerge as hostile attitudes become entrenched in powerful places, in the immediate future we'll more likely experience relational estrangement, victimization, job loss, and general marginalization.

WE MAY WONDER if all this will affect our lives. But persecution wears many faces.

Remember: the goal is to silence our voice and eliminate our influence. If this can be accomplished through threats, there's no need to turn up the heat. But if the "squeeze" on believers fails to achieve its desired end, beware. The pressure will escalate into ugly physical attacks attempting to close our mouths. Sin relentlessly runs this way.

We might anticipate persecution being first aimed at mature believers. While this makes sense logically, practically and historically it hasn't proved true. Almost immediately after his conversion, the apostle Paul faced persecution (Acts 9:23–25). While you may argue he wasn't your typical new believer, his converts faced the same suffering. Once Paul left town, the new believers usually experienced severe persecution.

Glenn Penner summarizes it well in his outstanding work on biblical persecution: "Persecution is not the lot just of dedicated, mature believers; it may also strike the weakest, youngest, oldest, and most vulnerable as well as the pillars of the local church."[10]

The goal is silencing believers' voices. Persecutors don't discriminate. Everyone who claims the name of Christ eventually lands in the crosshairs.

HOW CAN WE CONNECT
WITH TEACHING ON PERSECUTION?

This dramatic change in the American scenery places believers in uncomfortable and unfamiliar territory. As we've seen, in contrast to our brothers and sisters around the world, we have not been forced to live our faith in a hostile environment. We've enjoyed freedom and respect from broader society for our entire lives. With those privileges rapidly disappearing, we don't know how to respond.

Our theology is solid in other areas: We can articulate a sound theology of salvation and lead a friend to a saving faith in Christ. We express an orthodox ecclesiology and participate in the community life of a local church. But we aren't equipped to handle persecution because our environment—until now—hasn't given us an opportunity to personally apply the biblical texts.

What does this mean for preachers and leaders? Faithful preachers strive to apply the Word of God in relevant ways, but in a culture mostly devoid of persecution for believers, a challenge exists for the expositor of persecution passages. He may correctly understand the biblical principles and author's intentions, but the lives of his church members do not include unavoidable suffering for their faith. In a well-intentioned effort, the preacher often applies the passage to more general spiritual or psychological suffering.

I'm not criticizing; as a teaching pastor for almost two decades, I know the dance well. But because of this disparate cultural context, the American church has missed a vital element of discipleship. Important spiritual formation cannot be realized without experiencing suffering. Without this suffering, perseverance in the face of hardship remains theoretical. We can intellectually appreciate messages on "commitment despite the cost"—but without really experiencing what this means, such a call does not resonate.

Christ predicted persecution as His disciples struggled with the requirements of following Him. He called them to "deny themselves" and "take up their cross." He told them He was sending them "as lambs among wolves." He reminded them the world would "hate them just as it has hated Me." I suspect until the Passion Week the disciples were much like us—they heard Jesus' words and sought to understand them. But until they were actually experiencing these truths, the disciples—like us—couldn't quite connect with what their Teacher was saying.

Events in the book of Acts quickly remedied that. Christians experienced persecution immediately after Pentecost. Peter and John were arrested and threatened. Stephen became the first martyr. Hostility increased until the "gathered" church in Jerusalem became the "dispersed" church abroad as believers fled for safety throughout the region.

Many of the New Testament epistles share this backdrop. Peter writes to the "elect exiles of the Dispersion," believers indelibly marked by "fiery trials" (1 Pet. 1:7). James pens a letter to "the twelve tribes of the Dispersion" and calls upon them to "count it all joy . . . when you meet trials of various kinds" (James 1:2). The writer of Hebrews composes a lengthy letter to Jewish Christians considering a return to Judaism to escape persecution. He reminds them of "the former days when . . . you endured a hard struggle with sufferings, sometimes being publicly exposed to reproach and affliction" (Heb. 10:32–33).

While persecution is new terrain for American Christians, it's old terrain in the Bible. With our country's cultural shift, we have an opportunity to revisit the New Testament and learn how to apply the many passages on persecution in new ways.

Prepare will show you how.

OUR REALITY, GOD'S WORD,
AND REASONS FOR HOPE

To help you "prepare," I explore the new world we find ourselves in, take a look at what God's Word says, and conclude with a message of hope.

Part One: The New Reality. In two chapters, I briefly provide evidence of the dramatic cultural change in the United States and—to the best of my ability—explain how it occurred. While the shift has been radical, it hasn't been sudden. What we're experiencing is the fruit of a decades-long transformation. Many other books and websites provide hundreds of examples of the new reality, so I'll exercise restraint; my purpose isn't to alarm or sensationalize—just to identify today's cultural context lest some remain skeptical.

Part Two: Understanding Persecution: Five Counterintuitive Biblical Principles. We often have a truncated understanding of the Bible's teaching on persecution because of our inability to apply the texts. Part Two offers us a better grasp on biblical persecution by identifying five surprising principles often overlooked by American Christians. This is the heart of *Prepare*'s message.

Part Three: Reasons for Hope. The book's final section provides optimism for the future. I explain how all three persons of our triune God graciously help us when we face persecution. Included is a powerful and encouraging letter to American believers from a leader in the persecuted church in Pakistan. Finally, I consider the prospect of future spiritual revival and speculate on what it could mean if God chooses to revisit this land. And in an Afterword, I look at ways we can prepare ourselves spiritually—beginning now.

So *Prepare* ends with a message of hope. As children of the sovereign Lord of the universe, we must always cling to hope.

But we need to begin with a dose of reality. Whether you're a scoffer at the idea of persecution or firmly persuaded it's coming, I invite you to join me in a cultural tour of our country, the United States of America.

PART ONE

The New Reality

1

AWAKENING TO A DIFFERENT WORLD

But understand this, that in the last days there will come times of difficulty. For people will be lovers of self, lovers of money, proud, arrogant, abusive, disobedient to their parents, ungrateful, unholy, heartless, unappeasable, slanderous, without self-control, brutal, not loving good, treacherous, reckless, swollen with conceit, lovers of pleasure rather than lovers of God.

2 TIMOTHY 3:1–4

The fanciful tale of Rip Van Winkle surfaced posthumously in the papers of New York gentleman Diedrich Knickerbocker. Reflecting the region's Dutch heritage, Knickerbocker crafted a yarn about the work-averse, henpecked man named Rip Van Winkle. Rip lay down while squirrel hunting (his favorite activity) in the Kaatskill mountains. Not prone to vigorous activity and dulled by liquor, Rip fell into a deep sleep.

Twenty years later, when he woke up, he didn't realize he'd slept more than one night. But signs around him shouted he was in a whole new world. His snowy beard stretched a foot long. His dog, Wolf, had disappeared. His previously well-oiled rifle lay inoperative, encrusted with rust.

When he entered the village outskirts near his home, he didn't recognize it. His familiar haunts had disappeared, replaced by newer, larger buildings. The people dressed strangely and looked at him, with his twenty-year-old clothing, with suspicious curiosity. Bands of children hooted at him as he trudged the streets. Nothing looked the same. Rip's hometown held odd names, strange faces, and unfamiliar sights.

Many American believers today are having a similar experience. Maybe we haven't been physically asleep for twenty years, but we've been culturally asleep for forty. Insulated in our Christian subculture bubble and disconnected from the secular world, many of us have been largely unaware of society's movements. But events this past year awakened us. With our eyes wide open, we realize America's changed. As I mentioned in the introduction, the culture war is over—and we lost.[1]

With the battle decided, all that remains—as *New York Times* columnist Ross Douthat says—is "the terms of our surrender."[2] Those terms are still being negotiated, and two options exist. One choice means agreeing to disagree, peaceably coexist, and tolerate the other groups sharing our American turf. This is a plausible view, and *USA Today* columnist Oliver Thomas supports it.

> We may long for the day when people become more accepting of one another, but achieving that end by forcing people to violate their own conscience tears at the already frayed cords that bind us together as a nation. Call me Pollyanna, but I believe we can have equality for gays and lesbians *and* religious freedom. Contraceptive coverage for women *and* liberty of conscience. (italics original)[3]

This is a preferred approach, and it reflects the principles of freedom America was founded on. But as Douthat aptly observes, a second option is emerging: eliminate negotiation and force conformity. Wielding a painful but effective legal hammer, cultural activists silence believers' voices and dismantle any intrusive elements of the Christian subculture. We won't be invited to the table or called to peacefully coexist. Instead we're commanded to sit on the edges of society or risk punishment, lawsuits, and loss of our tax-exempt status. Douthat grimly states, "Now, apparently, the official line is that *you bigots don't get to negotiate anymore*." (italics original)[4]

Another conservative commentator—Erick Erickson—agrees with Douthat in his blog post "You Will Be Made to Care."

There will be no accommodation between gay rights activists and those seeking religious freedom to opt out of the gay rights movement. Gay rights activists demand tolerance for their lifestyle, but will not tolerate those who choose to adhere to their religious beliefs . . . Evil preaches tolerance until it is dominant and then it seeks to silence good. We are more and more rapidly arriving at a point in this country where Christians are being forced from the public square unless they abandon the tenets of their faith.[5]

While some Christians who kept their ear to the ground will support Erickson's conclusion, I recognize there are many others who—for a variety of reasons—remain skeptical. Perhaps your life hasn't been affected by the changes. Maybe you adopt the posture of the citizens of a state where I once lived: Missouri. You say, "Show Me."

> **WE WON'T BE invited to sit at the table or called to peacefully coexist.**

Let me present four game-changing developments that have already occurred. These aren't the only significant changes, and they certainly won't be the last. But as I write these words and survey the landscape, these are among the most important shifts.

ABANDONMENT OF BIBLICAL MARRIAGE

It's impossible to overstate the impact of the abandonment of biblical marriage. For all of America's (and humanity's) history, marriage has been defined by the biblical parameters: one man and one woman. This is God's design and, despite efforts to question the historic interpretation of the data,[6] it remains exegetically impregnable.

Ironically, our government passed the Defense of Marriage Act (HR3396; DOMA) in 1996 as a proactive measure ensuring traditional marriage remained the law.[7] DOMA established the federal definition of marriage as one man and one woman, and it passed in anticipation of Hawaii legally sanctioning same-sex marriages. Federal lawmakers feared this would create complicated issues for other states should a gay couple marry in Hawaii, move, and demand their marriage be recognized by the new state.

To subvert this complication, the bipartisan majorities of Congress passed DOMA, establishing no state or territory of the United States would be required to recognize any marriages outside a union between one man and one woman. President Bill Clinton signed the bill on September 20, 1996. A casual observer might assume this ended the debate.

Hardly. Gay-rights activists challenged the law, and the case (*United States v. Windsor*) eventually reached the Supreme Court in 2013. There, in a landmark 5–4 decision with Justice Anthony M. Kennedy joining the four liberal judges on the bench, the court overturned DOMA, rendering it null and void. The ruling declared that gay couples married in states where gay marriage is legal must receive the same federal health, tax, Social Security, and other benefits that heterosexual couples receive. In an unusual turnabout, Bill Clinton praised DOMA's demise. He wrote, "In 1996, I signed the Defense of Marriage Act. Although that was only 17 years ago, it was a very different time. In no state in the union was same-sex marriage recognized, much less available as a right, but some were moving that direction."[8]

Notice the cultural change Clinton acknowledges occurred in just seventeen years: "It was a very different time." A few months later, Bill and Hillary Clinton issued a joint statement. "By overturning the Defense of Marriage Act, the court recognized that discrimination towards any group holds us all back in our efforts to form a more perfect union."[9]

With this reversal by the Supreme Court, state legislatures rushed to pass laws legalizing gay marriage. Using the court's ruling as a legal barometer, some states—most notably on the West and East coasts—immediately sanctioned same-sex marriages. Others found their DOMA laws challenged in court, with activist judges granting temporary rights for gay couples to marry. When legal appeals from five states (Indiana, Oklahoma, Utah, Virginia and Wisconsin) reached the Supreme Court in October of 2014, the Court refused to intervene, effectively striking down gay marriage bans in those states and paving the way for six others to enact same-sex marriage. The ACLU called the action "a watershed moment for the entire country."[10]

The Supreme Court has not yet tackled the issue officially, but the strong message is that gay marriage could soon be legal across the country. In 2002, it was illegal for same-sex couples to marry anywhere in the country. At the writing of this book, over half of Americans now live in states that affirm gay marriage. Most legal experts expect the Supreme Court to soon accept a case that would settle the issue on a national basis. As it is, the recent refusal of the

Court to hear cases related to same-sex marriage opened the door to judges' ruling on gay marriage in several states.

How will this change affect believers holding a biblical view of marriage? We'll still be allowed to maintain and practice our "old view of marriage," but we won't be allowed to criticize gay marriage. Proof can be seen in several events that gained national notoriety. If we speak out, we'll be publicly vilified.

Brendan Eich found this out in a curious way. Eich, founder and CEO of Mozilla (maker of the Firefox browser), donated $1000 to support California's Proposition 8 ballot initiative affirming marriage between a man and a woman. This proposition passed with 52 percent of the vote, declaring gay marriage illegal in California. This was the sum of Eich's so-called crimes. He led his company with integrity and, according to other leaders at Mozilla, never displayed offensive behavior.

With the Supreme Court's abandonment of DOMA, California leaders chose not to defend Proposition 8; they immediately legalized same-sex marriages. Gay activists went on a witch hunt and discovered Eich's financial contribution to Proposition 8.

OVER HALF of all Americans now live in states that affirm gay marriage.

The website OkCupid decided to boycott Mozilla and called others to do likewise. The wireless company Credo Mobile gathered thousands of signatures demanding Eich's dismissal and put pressure on Mozilla's board of directors. After a few days, Eich resigned from his position and quietly stepped away. His resignation and job loss weren't because of incompetency but due to pressure from gay-marriage proponents who found his support of traditional marriage offensive.

Some called for a continuing purge of those opposed to same-sex marriage. William Saletan wrote, "Some of my colleagues are celebrating. They call Eich a bigot who got what he deserved. I agree. But let's not stop here. If we're serious about enforcing the new standard, thousands of other employees who donated to the same anti-gay ballot measure must be punished."[11]

Then Saletan upped the ante.

Thirty-seven companies in the database are linked to more than 1,300 employees who gave nearly $1 million in combined contributions to the campaign for Prop 8. Twenty-five tech companies are linked to 435 employees who gave more than $300,000. Many of these employees gave $1,000 apiece, if not more. Some, like Eich, are probably senior executives. Why do these bigots still have jobs? Let's go get them.[12]

Eich's resignation isn't an isolated incident. My hometown of Chicago witnessed a similar uprising in 2012 when Chick-fil-A president Dan Cathy expressed personal support for biblical marriage. Chick-fil-A had announced plans to build its second Chicago store in the trendy Logan Square neighborhood, but when Cathy's remarks became public, politics took center court.

Alderman Proco "Joe" Moreno went on record that he would block the company's efforts to build a store in his district: "If you are discriminating against a segment of the community, I don't want you in the 1st ward."[13] Moreno gained the support of Chicago mayor Rahm Emanuel who said, "The alderman has the ideological support of Mayor Rahm Emanuel. Chick-fil-A values are not Chicago values. They disrespect our fellow neighbors and residents. This would be a bad investment, since it would be empty."[14]

Neither Dan Cathy nor Chick-fil-A had discriminated against anyone in their employment practices or policies. Cathy only expressed a personal belief in biblical marriage. But this view is unacceptable to the broader culture. Far from being tolerant of contrary opinions, gay activists will seek to oppose and silence voices support-ing traditional marriage. Be forewarned.

Todd Starnes of Fox News sounds the alarm: "They [the gay rights community] not only expect you to accept their lifestyle, but they also want you to affirm it. They want your children exposed to it in their public school classrooms. They want private business owners to endorse their court-sanctioned 'marriages.' And woe be to any person who dares object."[15]

Erwin Lutzer declares, "The day of the casual Christian is over. No longer is it possible to drift along, hoping that no tough choices will have to be made."[16] Albert Mohler, president of The Southern Baptist Theological Seminary, sends the same message: "There will be no place to hide, and there will be no way to remain silent. To be silent will answer the question. The question is whether evangeli-cals will remain true to the teachings of Scripture and the unbroken teaching of the Christian church for over two thousand years on the morality of same-sex acts and the institution of marriage."[17]

EROSION OF RELIGIOUS FREEDOM

The second game-changing trend is the erosion of religious free-dom. Nothing is more precious to Americans than freedom. The Statue of Liberty stands boldly on the shores of our nation pro-claiming to the world that this is the land of the free. For over two centuries brave American soldiers have fought and died to protect our freedom.

While this liberty includes political freedom from totalitarian rulers, our nation's founders also ensured that it included religious freedom. The first line of the First Amendment in the United States Constitution is, "Congress shall make no law respecting an establish-ment of religion, or prohibiting the free exercise thereof."

But over the past few decades, religious freedom has been eroding. A Pew Research study rates the United States at a moderate level of restrictions in religious practices compared to other countries. In addition, the study indicates there's been a "marked increase" in hostility toward religion since 2009.[18] Since religious freedom and persecution operate in a converse relationship with each other, this guarantees tough days ahead for believers.

> **"THE DAY of the casual Christian is over."**

Congress sought to establish protection and parameters for religious freedom over twenty years ago. In response to a 1990 Oregon case (*Employment Division v. Smith*) that eliminated the requirement that government justify burdens on religious exercise imposed by laws, President Bill Clinton signed the Religious Freedom Restoration Act of 1993 (RFRA). This prohibited the government from burdening a person's exercise of religion unless there was a "compelling interest" by the government; and stated that a burden was the "least restrictive means" for enacting a neutral law to achieve said interest.

In other words, the RFRA was designed to protect the free exercise of religion while recognizing that certain activities under the guise of religion (e.g., murder, rape, assaults, etc.) aren't permissible because the government has a compelling interest in prohibiting them. This is reasonable, and no believer would argue against that premise. If a person claims their religious beliefs are being violated by a government regulation, RFRA requires a court to apply "strict scrutiny" to determine (1) if the religious beliefs are sincere, and (2) if the government has a genuine compelling interest in imposing the burden.

Despite the RFRA, our government continues to claw away our religious freedoms. One contemporary example is the Affordable Care Act (2010, ACA). Buried in the weighty web of new regulations is a mandate for employers to provide comprehensive contraception coverage in their employees' medical plans. This mandate includes all forms of contraception—including those understood to be abortifacient. To obey the ACA required Christians—who believe life begins at conception and must be protected—to compromise their beliefs. The governmental agency administering the ACA, Health and Human Services (HHS), provided no exceptions.

Religious groups, most notably the Roman Catholic Church, objected to the mandate under the provisions of the RFRA and were granted an exemption. But it created a serious ethical dilemma for other Christian-owned businesses who didn't qualify as religious organizations. Hobby Lobby, a chain of for-profit craft stores with 13,000 employees (owned by a family with evangelical beliefs), faced either the violation of the owners' religious beliefs or a $1.3-million-a-day fine for failing to comply. The company filed suit against the government (*Hobby Lobby v. Burwell*) using the legal tenets of the RFRA as its defense.

In June 2014 the Supreme Court voted 5–4, with Justice Samuel Alito writing the opinion. Hobby Lobby prevailed and gained the ability to follow its religious beliefs without penalty. While this case represents a victory for religious freedom, it was a narrow victory. The court specifically limited the ruling to closely held corporations with owners who have sincere religious beliefs. It cannot apply to other believers who share similar objections but not the narrow window. They will be forced to comply with the ACA despite their beliefs.

On the state level, the trend is also clearly pointing to further erosion of religious freedom. When a 1997 Supreme Court decision ruled RFRA inapplicable to state laws, states began enacting their own versions of the RFRA, including Arizona in 1999. In early 2014 the Arizona state legislature passed an amendment to RFRA (SB 1062) allowing businesses involved in public accommodation the ability to use RFRA as a defense if they were sued for discrimination. It didn't allow for greater discrimination, as falsely reported; it simply provided defendants with sincere religious beliefs the ability to appeal to the state's RFRA in a lawsuit.

The gay rights community immediately applied intense pressure to Arizona governor Jan Brewer; they condemned the bill as anti-gay and discriminatory. The National Football League added economic pressure, threatening to move the Super Bowl from Arizona if the amendment became law.[19] Major corporations such as Apple, Delta, and American Airlines voiced opposition.[20] Caving to the pressure, Governor Brewer vetoed the bill.[21]

In the wake of these religious freedom issues are believers facing painful decisions. Owners of any public business, be it a bakery,[22] a florist,[23] or a photography studio,[24] will be forced to decide if they'll put their values on a shelf, close up shop, or prepare for a lawsuit.

Brian Walsh, executive director of the American Religious Freedom Program, gives this warning: "There have been decades of assurances that if same-sex marriage becomes law, it would not restrict religious freedom. A lot of people took those assurances at face value. I would say those assurances are being called into question."[25] George Neumayr predicts, "It will be the death of religious freedom by a thousand little cuts here and there; cancelled speeches of religious figures at state universities, lost HHS grants, the refusal of city governments to recognize churches that don't permit gay marriages, 'hate crime' legislation that extends to opposition to gay marriage, and so on."[26]

PROTECTION OF SPECIAL INTEREST GROUPS

Unlike the previously mentioned changes, the protection of special interest groups—specifically the lesbian, gay, bisexual, and transgendered (LGBT) community—is an avalanche just beginning. When this wave reaches full strength, its impact will be far-reaching.

The issue is the practice of discrimination. The Bible strongly objects to sinful discrimination based on external appearances (e.g., James 2:1–13). American church history is replete with spiritual justification for the enslavement and abuse of African Americans. We must not repeat those tragic sins.

But despite efforts to equate the discrimination against the LGBT community with the enslavement of African Americans, the issues are fundamentally different. While there's nothing sinful about having black or white skin, the Bible says homosexual behavior and changing one's gender is wrong—an affront to the Creator (Lev. 18:22; 20:13; Rom. 1:26–27). Yet in the near future, laws could require churches and religious nonprofits to hire gay and transgender individuals—or face a lawsuit. Gordon College, an evangelical school in Massachusetts with a policy forbidding homosexual practice for students and staff, has been warned its policy may run afoul of accreditation standards. Gordon president D. Michael Lindsay, citing the importance of religious freedom, noted that faith-based colleges must have the freedom to "set the conditions for community life." The accrediting agency responsible for evaluating the school requires institutions to pursue "nondiscriminatory" policies in employment and other areas of campus life.[27] Gordon has been given a year to "review" its policy. Emboldened, other accrediting agencies may enforce similar standards on other Christian schools across the country.

Federal lawmakers are being pressured by the White House to pass the Employment Non-Discrimination Act (ENDA). This proposed legislation would make it illegal for employers to discriminate on the basis of sexual orientation or gender identity. The Senate passed the ENDA, but the law has remained stalled in the Republican-controlled House of Representatives. In light of the Hobby Lobby decision, some LGBT leaders have withdrawn support for the ENDA, wanting it to be reworked to eliminate religious loopholes.[28] It appears that, while the passage of the ENDA may not be imminent, at some time and in some form it will pass.

In July of 2014 President Obama signed an executive order (amendment to orders 11478 and 11246) with more limited reach.[29]

The order bars federal contractors from discriminating against employees on the basis of sexual orientation or gender identity. It doesn't include a religious exemption, despite calls from Catholic and evangelical leaders. Therefore, any religious organization with federal contracts cannot require employees to abide by their faith's teachings, which compromises the organization's spiritual integrity.

The resulting cultural collision greatly exceeds the stir caused by the ACA. As schools, churches, and nonprofit religious organizations with federal contracts consider new employees, they can't discriminate against those involved in a gay lifestyle or who surgically changed their gender.

HOSTILE ATTITUDES TOWARD CHRISTIANITY

If you're under age forty, it may not seem like the culture has significantly changed, but in the eyes of those in our forties, fifties, and beyond? It's been dramatic. I entered into vocational Christian ministry in 1983 after college and seminary. Back then our culture still embraced and promoted biblical values—at least officially. You could identify yourself as a Christian, publicly pray in Jesus' name, and hold Bible studies on college campuses.

Now the environment is hostile. Now we are told our views aren't welcome. Now we're hated. We're lumped into the same bigoted, narrow category as Donald Sterling, the former owner of the Los Angeles Clippers. Researcher George Barna, in his book *Futurecast*, writes, "Americans are becoming more hostile and negative toward Christianity."[30]

John Dickerson correctly noted that the size of the evangelical church is much smaller than some have projected. Multiple surveys peg the number of evangelicals in the range of eighteen to twenty million[31]—roughly 5–6 percent of the population. With an increasingly shrinking minority status, Christians are being ordered to leave the room and take their Bible talk with them.

At the University of North Carolina-Wilmington, a professor of criminology named Mike Adams was hired and gained promotions and tenure while he was a self-described atheist. In 2000, he had a radical conversion to Christ and became outspoken about his faith. Despite strong evaluations and two faculty awards, Mike was denied promotion to full professor in 2010. After a four-year fight in the courts, a US District Court judge ruled in his favor and required the university to not only promote him but also award him $50,000 in back pay.[32]

At the United States Air Force Academy a cadet started a firestorm by writing Galatians 2:20 on the whiteboard outside his room: "I have been crucified with Christ. It is no longer I who live, but Christ who lives in me." Complaints were lodged and Mikey Weinstein, director of the Military Religious Freedom Foundation, pressed the case against the cadet. "It clearly elevated one religious faith (fundamentalist Christianity) over all others at an already virulently hyper-fundamentalist Christian institution. It massively poured fundamentalist Christian gasoline on an already raging out-of-control conflagration of fundamentalist Christian tyranny, exceptionalism and supremacy at the USAFA."[33]

> **WITH AN increasingly shrinking minority status, Christians are being ordered to leave the room and take their Bible talk with them.**

Can you detect hostility in those words? It's raging. And it worked. Two hours after the complaints were received, the cadet's commanding officer ordered him to remove the verse. Ironically, the same brass that removed the Scripture verse and denied cadets participation in Operation Christmas Child with Samaritan's Purse allowed the Academy-approved cadet Freethinkers Club to sponsor "Ask an Atheist Day."[34]

At Maxwell Air Force Base in Alabama new military recruits can no longer be personally given Bibles by the Gideons International Bible Society. This practice, in place for over a decade, allowed Gideon volunteers to shake hands with new recruits after they finished their required paperwork and offer them a pocket-sized Bible. Volunteer Michael Fredenburg said, "They kicked us out. They told us, 'get your Bibles out.' "[35] They now allow a display table with materials, but they prohibit the personal distribution.

The Bible disappeared from the POW/MIA Missing Man Table at Patrick Air Force Base in Florida. The Missing Man Table, established to honor the plight of military personnel who are missing in action or prisoners of war, includes a white tablecloth setting with an inverted glass, a plate with lemon and salt, a single rose, a candle, and a Bible. Each element was outlined in the official ceremony brochure. In early 2014 someone objected to the Bible and it was removed. The Air Force explained why:

> The 45th Space Wing deeply desires to honor America's Prisoners of War (POW) and Missing in Action (MIA) personnel. Unfortunately, the Bible's presence or absence at the table at the Riverside Dining Facility ignited controversy and division, distracting from the table's primary purpose of honoring POWs/MIAs. Consequently, we temporarily replaced the table with the POW/MIA flag in an effort to show our continued support of these heroes while seeking an acceptable solution to the controversy.[36]

Examples abound of students at all levels of public schools encountering hostility for praying or carrying Bibles to school. In one instance, two middle-school sisters carried their Bibles to

IT'S PAINFUL for me to admit that the country I love has radically changed.

school and their teacher confiscated them and called the girls' mother, threatening to turn the girls over to Child Protective Services. When the mother arrived at school the teacher threw the Bibles into the trash and said, "This is garbage!"[37]

The growing hostility against Christians, Christianity, and the Bible is evident across the country. Starnes reports countless stories:

- A Sonoma State University student must remove her two-inch-tall cross necklace because her supervisor believed it would offend other students.[38]
- A first-grade student in North Carolina is ordered to remove the word *God* from a poem she was supposed to read on Veteran's Day in honor of her two grandfathers, who served in Vietnam.[39]
- A New Jersey school district banned all religious Christmas music, requiring every song at their winter concerts to be secular.[40]
- An Army email labeled pro-family Christian ministries as "Domestic Hate Groups," listing them with the Ku Klux Klan and Neo-Nazis.[41]
- Evangelical pastor Louie Giglio was ousted from the 2012 presidential inauguration program because he delivered a sermon in the 1990s calling the practice of homosexuality sin.[42]

These aren't isolated stories—they're part of a national trend. Hundreds of stories could fill this space.[43] It's painful for me to admit that the country I love has radically changed, and the pace of change is accelerating. Followers of Jesus who awakened from a cultural sleep are facing hostility, rejection, and marginalization. The trend lines point to increased opposition—including genuine persecution.

Since persecution is on our future menu and we need to understand it, I will explain in chapters 3 through 7 what the Bible teaches. But first let's examine how America arrived at this place.

2

CROSSING THE RUBICON

In those days there was no king in Israel.
Everyone did what was right in his own eyes.

JUDGES 21:25

In 49 BC a popular, powerful new leader was emerging in the Roman Empire. Blessed with extraordinary oratory skills, outstanding military prowess, and unbridled political ambition, Julius Caesar had already made a rapid rise through the political ranks. Ten years earlier he'd started as consul of Rome. A year later he became governor of Gaul, where he powerfully subdued the native Celtic and Germanic tribes. With his immense popularity making him a threat to Rome and Pompey, the Senate called him to resign his command and disband his army—or risk being labeled an enemy of the state.

From his home in Ravenna, north of Rome, Caesar pondered his options. Either he yielded to the Senate command, or he mobilized his army to move south and engage in a bloody fight with Pompey for control of the empire. Roman law forbade any military leader passing the Rubicon River with a standing army. To do so meant treason. Crossing the river would signal a point of no return.

Driven by his passion to lead Rome, Caesar led a single legion of men to the banks of the river where, according to some historians, he hesitated. But then he sounded the trumpet, cried out the famous Latin phrase *alea iacta est*—which means "the die has been cast"— and led his army across the river. His decisive act caused Pompey and a large part of the Senate to flee from Rome in fear, and Caesar eventually became the emperor.[1]

In our American culture war we have crossed the Rubicon. The die has been cast, the tipping point reached. Barring a gracious visitation from God, this nation is not going back to the culture and values it held in the past. The war is over, and the immediate future for believers will involve learning how to live righteously in this new environment—not pining for the good old days.

This begs the question: how did this happen? And when? Perhaps we have been guilty of overlooking the changes that have occurred, but if the war is over it's helpful to engage in a cultural postmortem. How did America get here?

As I hinted before, the change didn't happen overnight. The highly individualized, relativistic, anti-Christian culture we endure today was not a product of lightning-fast changes, but a slow, methodical, extremely effective transformation occurring over several decades. While I'm not a social scientist, I've sought to understand how cultural change occurs and specifically what happened in America. Let me try to explain this in terms we can understand.

HOW CULTURAL CHANGE HAPPENS

The United States Constitution is the most important legal document in our country. It's based on both biblical and British common-law principles, as found eloquently expressed in 1765 by Sir William Blackstone in a series of books called *Commentaries on the Laws of England.*

Blackstone had argued—and America's founders agreed—"that

judges were not 'delegated to pronounce a new law, but to maintain and expound the old one.' "[2] This old law, which judges were to find and interpret in each particular case, was the law God set in place when He created the universe. It's unchanging and "binding over all the globe, in all countries, and at all times."[3] America's foundational legal system was based upon this understanding that God alone has the authority to impose His law on His created subjects.[4] Titus states, "Blackstone's *Commentaries* soon became the basic textbook for teaching law. For generations . . . most American lawyers learned law by reading Blackstone."[5] This approach taught that "judges did not make the common law, they only discovered, stated, and applied it. A judge's opinion or order in a particular case, therefore was not . . . law; it was only evidence of law."[6]

Since its composition more than two centuries ago, the Constitution has changed very little. It sets forth the nature and extent of the liberties to be enjoyed by America's citizens—freedoms consistent with biblical principle. Obviously, with the massive cultural changes sweeping across our country, while the Constitution's words haven't changed, the way it's interpreted has. How did this happen?

To answer that we first need to understand what culture is. The best definition I found is "a culture is a way of life for a group of people—the behaviors, beliefs, values and symbols that they accept, generally without thinking about them, and that are passed along by communication and imitation from one generation to the next."[7]

In short, *a culture is how and why people do things.* Culture is complex—it includes all human behavior and institutions, such as popular entertainment, art, education, law, religion, morality, economic activity, and technology. It's also fluid not static.

Culture changes when people are exposed to a new idea, thought, or invention that seems preferable to them and is enfolded into the society. This follows a predictable, five-step process I can illustrate using the example of the abolition of slavery.

Step One: A Contact Happens

Cultural change begins with *diffusion*: that is, people within the culture have contact with a new thought, value, invention, or idea. In Christian missions this happened as missionaries went around the world proclaiming the gospel to those who had never heard it. With slavery, diffusion began when Americans became aware of William Wilberforce's abolitionist views.

America practiced slavery from the founding of our country to the middle of the nineteenth century. At that time our culture's beliefs and values included an acceptance of blacks being bought, sold, and subjugated. That view began to change with exposure to England's Wilberforce.

Step Two: A Champion Emerges

From an initial contact with a new idea comes a *champion* for the idea. This person becomes the driving force for bringing change. With slavery, the obvious champion for abolition in America was President Abraham Lincoln. Although he paid a high price for his beliefs—eventually being assassinated—he is revered for his leadership in ending slavery—and preserving the Union. The champion need not be a political figure, but they must possess the influence to lead the desired change.

Step Three: A Coalition Builds

A change in how and why people do things requires more than a champion to be successful. There must be a growing *coalition* of people within the culture who join forces with the champion. In the case of slavery, Lincoln was joined by abolitionists Frederick Douglass, John Brown, and Harriett Beecher Stowe (among others). The forces of abolitionism had been fighting for an end to slavery for many years. Eventually, of course, the battles over slavery and states' rights led to the outbreak of the Civil War.

In the change process, a societal milestone eventually occurs which serves as a tipping point. A contact has been made, a champion has emerged, and a coalition is built, leading to the tipping point. This is when the Rubicon is usually crossed.

Step Four: A Law Is Passed

Supreme Court Justice nominee Robert Bork once said, "Culture eventually makes politics."[8] He meant that the values of a culture become cemented into a society when they're politicized—when they become the law of the land. This creates a new norm for the society. With our example, this happened with the passing of the Sixteenth Amendment to the US Constitution, outlawing slavery.

Step Five: An Integration Occurs

After a law is passed and the cultural change is politicized, society adjusts to the new reality and begins to reflect the new value. The integration is usually gradual, with some portions of society adapting easier and faster than others. Ultimately the integration is complete, and the previous cultural value fades into the history books. With slavery, the integration continued through a series of societal adjustments and laws to prevent racial discrimination. This continues today; while slavery isn't practiced, we still see evidence of racism.

Since cultures are never static, this change process is cyclical, not linear. Here is a possible way to chart the process.

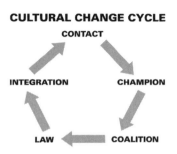

CULTURAL CHANGE CYCLE

CULTURAL CHANGE AND RELIGIOUS FREEDOM

If you will grant me the model I've presented, we can track the same process of cultural change with religious freedom. The original culture, as envisioned by the framers of the Constitution, ensured maximum freedom for all—including religious freedom. But this has been changing.

1. A Contact Happens

The new, disruptive thought introduced into American society was Darwinian evolutionism. Charles Darwin published *On the Origin of Species* in 1859. The idea of a godless, evolutionary system using incremental change to progress from simple life to complex beings changed the thinking of many disciplines, including law. In the legal arena this meant a nation could determine its own law and govern its own affairs—without God.

When Charles William Eliot was appointed president of Harvard University in 1869, he'd already been heavily influenced by evolutionary thought, and he assumed the key to knowledge was man's observation under the discipline of a scientific mind, not God's revelation under the discipline of the Holy Spirit.[9]

Oliver Wendell Holmes Jr., as Associate Jurist on the Supreme Court, wrote a dissenting opinion in 1917 reflecting these views. "The common law is not a brooding omnipresence in the sky [based on God], but the articulate voice of some [earthly] sovereign, or quasi-sovereign that can be identified."[10] Beginning in the late 1800s Holmes and other legal scholars repeatedly argued for a new approach to the legal system: one in which the objective isn't discovering God's law—as Blackstone had set forth in his *Commentaries*—but man's law, which evolved through time.[11]

2. A Champion Emerges

Before 1850 most lawyers weren't trained in law school, but as apprentices in law offices.[12] Harvard, with an early law school, was the first American university to incorporate Darwinian principles into all the academic disciplines, including law. Wanting to instill an evolutionary approach, President Eliot appointed Christopher Columbus Langdell as the new dean at Harvard's law school in 1870.[13]

Langdell shared Eliot's belief in Darwinism. They also shared a desire to treat law as a science to be discoverable through inductive reasoning processes. From this perch, Langdell revolutionized legal education at Harvard and throughout the United States by creating a case method approach of teaching law. [14]

The case method, inherently evolutionary and dramatically different from the discovery of divine law set forth by William Blackstone, required students to collect and study opinions written by judges in legal cases. From these cases, using human reason, generalized laws could be extracted. Therefore, under Langdell, Harvard trained lawyers to practice progressive, evolutionary law (i.e., not static, adapting to the needs of man and society).

3. A Coalition Builds

It took several decades for the legal profession to be transformed by this new approach to interpreting the law, but soon progressive lawyers and jurists dominated the industry. Attorney David Gibbs III of the National Center for Life and Liberty writes,

> After Harvard's new approach to legal education was implemented in the 1870s, it took another 40 or 50 years for these law students to set up their practices and begin to dominate America's legal circles. Groups like the Humanist Society and the American Civil Liberties Union, organized during the 1920s, helped to expedite the process. It then took another 20 years or more

for these progressive lawyers to begin receiving appointments as judges, and finally, by the 1960s, to dominate the United States Supreme Court.[15]

The 1960s was also when postmodernism began to take root, bringing a rejection of absolutes and an acceptance of relativism. Postmodern epistemology replaced modernism, with devastating results. Scholar D. A. Carson explains the difference:

Modernist epistemology taught us that in every discipline, and in thought itself, there are certain universal foundations on which we can build with methodological rigor; postmodern epistemology insists that both the foundations and the methods are culturally contrived, and therefore the resulting "knowledge" is necessarily the function of particular cultures.[16]

A postmodern mindset added fuel to the progressivism of the legal arena, creating a powerful coalition. The tipping point came in 1947, when the Supreme Court reinterpreted the Establishment Clause in the landmark case *Everson v. Board of Education.* The Establishment Clause, found in the First Amendment, states the federal government should "make no law respecting an establishment of religion."[17]

This clause's meaning was never in question until progressive jurists took the bench in the middle of the twentieth century. In the Everson case, the Supreme Court expanded the federal law to apply to state and local jurisdictions.[18] It also turned the clause upside down, stating a "high and impregnable" wall of separation exists between church and state, and the state must be protected from the church.[19]

4. A Law Is Passed

Many laws have been passed in the past fifty years to cement this new value into America's culture. Here are a few of the more significant cases.

Engel v. Vitale (1962)[20]

Prayer and Bible reading were removed from the public schools, deemed a violation of the Establishment Clause.

Roe v. Wade (1973)[21]

This famous case naturally grew from the court's movement toward individualism and privacy. The right to contraception for both married couples and singles had been established in previous cases. With this ruling, resulting in the murder of millions of innocent children, women were given the constitutional right to have an abortion.

Stone v. Graham (1980)[22]

The court decided a picture of the Ten Commandments hanging in a school hallway violated the Establishment Clause, and they removed the Ten Commandments from public schools.

Planned Parenthood v. Casey (1992)[23]

The court overturned the old requirement for minors to gain parental consent for an abortion, allowing them an abortion without a form of permission ("judicial bypass") granted by the judge. In its ruling the court gave new definition to individual liberty. Gibbs writes,

> The United States Supreme Court in its 1992 *Casey* decision completely changed that Divine orientation [that men and women were endowed by their Creator with certain unalienable rights] and ruled that the constitutional right to "liberty" is so expansive that "at the heart of liberty is the right to define one's own concept of existence, of meaning, of the universe and of the mystery of human life." In other words, liberty is no longer dependent upon the heavenly Absolute Sovereign recognized by our founders in the Declaration of Independence.[24]

Romer v. Evans (1996)[25]

The court gave a major decision for the gay community by deciding that a Colorado state constitutional initiative that denied special rights for homosexuals and bisexuals was unconstitutional. This provided the legal precedent for gays to gain protected status as a minority group.

Lawrence v. Texas (2003)[26]

Building on the 1996 *Romer v. Evans* decision, this ruling provided the legal foundation for gay marriage as we know it today by striking down a Texas state law making sodomy a crime.

> In the 2003 sodomy criminal case of *Lawrence v. Texas*, the Supreme Court followed up its 1996 decision and moved the ball even farther down the field. By using the same sort of runaway autonomy first signaled in the Casey [decision] the court . . . laid the legal groundwork for gay marriage, as well as perhaps for any other sort of marriage or civil union any couple or group might want to put together to claim traditional governmental benefits traditionally only extended to God-ordained marriage and family.[27]

United States v. Windsor (2013)[28]

We referred to this case in chapter 1, when the court struck down the DOMA and restricted the federal interpretation of *marriage* and *spouse* to only refer to heterosexual unions. *United States v. Windsor* removed any federal barrier to the legalization of gay marriage. At the time of the *Windsor* decision, Associate Justice Antonin Scalia predicted our present states' rush to recognize same-sex marriages. He said, "It takes real cheek for today's majority to assure us, as it is going out the door, that a constitutional requirement to give formal recognition to same-sex marriage is not at issue here . . . the majority arms well every challenger to a state law restricting marriage to its traditional definition."[29] Unfortunately, Scalia proved prophetic.

5. Integration Occurs

Finally comes the adjustment phase as our society adapts to the new reality. The transformation has been rapid; polls show a strong shift in citizens' opinions of gay marriage—in a short time period.

Gallup

A Gallup poll shows that twice as many Americans in 2014 believe same-sex marriages should be legal than did in 1996. They were asked, "Do you think marriages between same-sex couples should or should not be recognized by the law as valid, with the same rights as traditional marriages?"

When they took the poll in March of 1996, 27 percent said same-sex marriages should be valid, and 68 percent said they shouldn't. But by July of 2014, 55 percent of respondents said same-sex marriage should be valid, and 42 percent said they shouldn't.[30]

Do you think marriages between same-sex couples should or should not be recognized by the law as valid, with the same rights as traditional marriages?

■ % Should be valid ▨ % Should not be valid

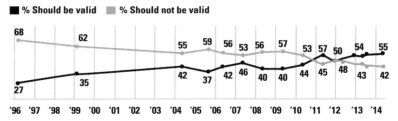

Note: Trend shown for pools in which same-sex marriage question followed questions on gay/lesbian rights and relations
1996–2006 wording: "Do you think marriages between homosexuals . . ."

GALLUP

While the increased support for gay marriage is expected, it can be projected to go higher as our country's demographics change and the older, more conservative generations die. Gallup's poll showed a much more favorable attitude toward gay marriage among young people versus older; nearly eight out of every ten people under age thirty affirm gay marriage.

Support for Legal Same-Sex Marriage by Age, 1996, 2013, and 2014

	% Should be legal, 1996	% Should be legal, 2013	% Should be legal, 2014	Change, 1996–2014 (pct. pts.)
18 to 29 years	41	70	78	+37
30 to 49 years	30	53	54	+24
50 to 64 years	15	46	48	+33
65+ years	14	41	42	28

GALLUP

It is vital to see there's been a dramatic change in the attitude toward same-sex marriage among all age groups, not just among young people. Three times as many Americans over the age of 65 believed gay marriage should be legal than did in 1996. This shows a culture integrating changes.

Bloomberg

A Bloomberg National Poll, conducted by Selzer & Company in March 2014, yielded nearly identical statistics to the Gallup poll.[31] It asked one thousand adults across America:

3/7–10/14

Do you support or oppose allowing same-sex couples to get married?

Support	Oppose	Unsure
55%	36%	9%

ABC News/Washington Post

A poll conducted by ABC News and the *Washington Post* in June 2014 shows only slightly higher numbers.[32] It asked one thousand adults:

5/29–6/1/14

Overall, do you support or oppose allowing gays and lesbians to marry legally?

Support	Oppose	Unsure
56%	38%	9%

While all trends like this have a measure of momentum behind them, even pollsters recognize the changes are historic. Alex Lundry served as the director of data science for the 2012 Mitt Romney presidential campaign and now works for the market research firm Target-Point. As he analyzed the speed of the change, he commented, "This is moving faster than any issue we've ever tracked. This is the future talking to us."[33] What's driving this change? Personal contact with gay family members, gay friends, and gay neighbors. Lundry said activists are winning the battle for "the hearts and minds of people."[34]

THE POLITICAL SHIFT

Robert Bork said "culture gets politicized" and "politics gets culturized," meaning both feed off each other. As the cultural change gets embedded through the legal and political process, the politicians reflect the new reality in their views or face losing their seat of power. The Democratic Party has been historically more receptive to gay rights and gay marriage but, with the cultural integration, Republican Party lawmakers are rapidly changing their views.

In an April 2014 article in the *Washington Post*, political analysts agreed that "a tectonic shift is taking place in the Republican Party on marriage equality."[35] A spokesman for the Human Rights

Campaign, a gay rights group, said, "For the Republican hierarchy, it's a very straightforward question: how can they attract the next generation of voters and not support an issue young people have made their minds up on?"[36]

> **A SINGLE change in the judiciary makes any protection of religious freedom unlikely.**

As younger Republicans gain additional clout, the question will be quickly settled. A Pew Research Poll shows young Republicans, like most young Americans, strongly favor gay marriage.[37]

Between younger Republicans and older Republicans there is a 39-percentage-point difference. The handwriting is on the wall. The Republican Party will eventually mirror the Democrats, and gay marriage will be completely politicized.

At this moment, integration continues with increased momentum. Other issues will follow on the heels of gay marriage as the full implications of this cultural change works itself out in our society. A host of transgender issues will be debated. States are already wrestling with restroom issues for the transgendered,[38] but the cascading issues will become complex, including birth certificates, marriage certificates, and even school diplomas.

As the culture further integrates, expect more rulings from the Supreme Court increasingly restricting religious freedom. The current Supreme Court is ideologically divided with four liberal, progressive judges, four conservative, statutory judges, and one judge serving as a swing vote. A single change in the judiciary—i.e., the loss of one conservative vote to retirement or death—makes any protection of religious freedom unlikely.

The question remains: is gay marriage the logical end to our cultural change? With privacy and individualism reigning supreme in our courts, and with a relativistic philosophy devoid of absolutes

MOST YOUNG REPUBLICANS FAVOR
SAME-SEX MARRIAGE

*Percent who favor allowing gays
and lesbians to marry legally*

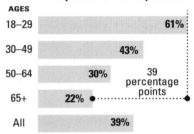

Republican/Lean Republican

AGES

18–29	61%
30–49	43%
50–64	30%
65+	22%
All	39%

39 percentage points

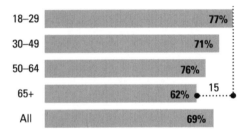

Democrat/Lean Democrat

18–29	77%
30–49	71%
50–64	76%
65+	62%
All	69%

15

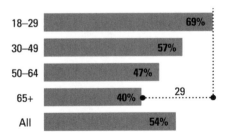

Total

18–29	69%
30–49	57%
50–64	47%
65+	40%
All	54%

29

PEW RESEARCH CENTER

dominating intellectuals around the country, what else could we see in this country in the name of "marriage"? Is polygamy wrong? Is incest out of the question? Os Guinness states, "As the legalization and then normalization of polyamory, polygamy, pedophilia, and incest follow the same logic as that of abortion and homosexuality, the socially destructive consequences of these trends will reverberate throughout society until the social chaos is beyond recovery."[39]

The future prospects cause me to shudder. It is clear we have crossed the Rubicon. The die has been cast. The tipping point has been reached. We have lost the war.

What now?

We need not be pessimists, but we must be realists. Realism shows that with the current, accelerating trends in America, we can expect our voices to be silenced. We can expect to be persecuted for our views. We can expect to be rejected and punished in the land of the free—for standing on scriptural truth.

Since this is a new experience for nearly all of us, we need to understand what the Bible says about persecution. The verses that didn't apply to us before will take on new meaning. Let's move into Part 2 and discover five counterintuitive biblical principles on persecution.

PART TWO

Understanding Persecution— Five Counterintuitive Biblical Principles

3

NORMAL NOT STRANGE

Beloved, do not be surprised at the fiery trial
when it comes upon you to test you, as though
something strange were happening to you.

1 PETER 4:12

The two disciples trudged down the road, struggling to process recent events. Like throngs of others, they had been in Jerusalem to celebrate Passover, but the celebration turned into a funeral. Their beloved teacher—the one they considered the Messiah—Jesus of Nazareth—had been crucified.

The chief priests and scribes had arrested Him the day before Passover and charged Him with blasphemy. A circus of trials ensued before both the Jewish leaders and the Roman authorities. In the end, they condemned Jesus. Hung on a cross between two thieves He died, and friends buried Him before sundown on Friday.

As they continued their journey, the two disciples—Cleopas and his wife—kept talking about the unexpected events. They thought Jesus was the one promised to bring redemption to Israel. They believed He would lead them in finally casting off the hated rule of the Romans. Now that He had died, they didn't know what to think.

It was now Sunday. Just before Cleopas and his wife left Jerusalem to return to Emmaus, a strange report came from some of the women who had visited Jesus' tomb. His body was missing! An angel had told them Jesus was alive. Others—including Peter and John—made a hasty trip to the grave to verify the story. The truth made them reel. Jesus' tomb had been opened, and His body had vanished.

With all this transpiring in the last few days, the two travelers didn't lack a topic of conversation. They hardly noticed when a stranger joined them. Seeking to join the discussion, the newcomer asked, "What is this conversation that you are holding with each other as you walk?"

Stunned by His perceived ignorance, they stopped dead and looked at Him sadly. They asked if He was the only person in Israel unaware of what had happened in Jerusalem. When He asked, "What things?" they vividly recounted their version of the events, probably expecting the stranger to add little to their report.

How wrong they were. The man who had joined them, Jesus, responded to their interpretation of the past few days by saying, "O foolish ones, and slow of heart to believe all that the prophets had spoken! Was it not necessary that the Christ should suffer these things and enter into his glory?" (Luke 24:25–26)

Jesus followed this opening salvo with a walk through the pages of the Bible, as He explained how what had transpired concerning Him fulfilled Scripture starting with Moses and the prophets. How I would have loved to hear those words!

Notice that the disciples had missed the necessity of Christ's suffering. This is instructive for us. As Jesus explained to them, the prophets predicted such suffering, yet in their passion to see a conquering king and not a suffering servant, they had missed it.

As American Christians, we have the same blind spots as Cleopas and his wife. We don't expect suffering and persecution as Christians. Living in a culture with strong Judeo-Christian roots, we expect our lives to be marked by general prosperity and societal acceptance. Persecution is strange.

But biblically, it's reversed. This is the first counterintuitive principle from Scripture about persecution: *the persecution of believers is normal, not strange.*

THE WORLD HATES US

One of the more difficult truths for us to grasp is that the world hates us. The world doesn't tolerate us—even though toleration is a supposed value of our society. It doesn't like us. No, it hates us. Jesus makes this plain in John 15:18–27.

His statement in John 15 is found in the middle of a long sermon we often call the Upper Room Discourse (John 14–17). The message begins in the upper room after Jesus celebrated the Passover with His disciples. At the end of chapter 14, Jesus calls them to leave the room, and they begin walking through Jerusalem, skirting the Temple Mount on their way to the garden of Gethsemane.

As they walk, knowing that in just a few hours He would be betrayed and arrested, Jesus talks about the extreme hostility His disciples will face. Seven times in this passage—which consists of just ten verses—He says they'll face hatred. Repetition in the Bible is important; it always communicates emphasis. Jesus' sevenfold use of *hate* shows His emphasis. We, His followers, can expect to be hated.

> **IN THEIR passion to see a conquering king, the disciples missed the necessity of Christ's suffering.**

The passage begins in verse 18 with a sharp contrast to the previous section. In John 15:12–17 Jesus talks about the disciples' relationships to each other. The key word in those verses is *love*. He concludes verse 17 by saying, "These things I command you, so that you will love one another." But then, instructing the disciples about their relationship with the world, He says, "If the world hates you, know that it has hated me before it hated you" (v. 18).

That verse can be confusing unless you understand the kind of conditional statement Jesus used. The Greek language is marvelously flexible, containing several different ways of making a conditional statement. This one assumes the reality of what is stated. When He says, "If the world hates you," He is saying, "*Since* the world hates you," or "If the world hates you, as it does . . ." His goal is that we accept reality: the world hates us. To reinforce this, Jesus repeats the same thought in verse 19. "I chose you out of the world, therefore the world hates you."

Obviously, *hate* is a strong word. It's a relational word—the polar opposite of love. When speaking of a relationship between people, *hate* means there is extreme animosity between them. Here the hostility is between us and the world. The world hates us.

But who is the "world"? Who hates us?

The Greek word used for *world* (*cosmos*) doesn't refer to the physical earth or its inhabitants. It refers to the ungodly system permeating the earth, which is hostile toward God and shakes its fists at Him at every turn. The world's beliefs and values are antagonistic to God, His Word, and His people. This is the system Paul commands us to avoid when he writes in Romans 12:2, "Do not be conformed to this world, but be transformed by the renewal of your mind."

This is the world.

God says marriage is between a man and a woman; the world says that's unnecessary. It can be between two men or two women.

God says, "I give grace to the humble"; the world says, "Only a fool stoops down. You have to claw and fight to get ahead—even if it destroys others."

God says riches are a snare that can bring destruction; the world says accumulating money is life's end goal—and the one who has the gold makes the rules.

This is the world. And Jesus says the world hates us.

Fortunately, we're not alone as objects of this hate. Before the world hated us, it hated Christ. He reminds us of this: "If the world hates you [as it does], know that it has hated me before it hated you" (v. 18). In this verse, Jesus uses a present tense verb indicating a continuing condition. This means the world hated Christ in the past, hates Him in the present, and will continue to hate Him in the future.

But the hate extends even further. The world hates us, the world hates Christ, and the world also hates God. In John 15:23 Jesus says, "Whoever hates me hates my Father also."

Do they hate Christ? Yes.

Do they hate the Father? Absolutely. Jesus confirms this when He says, "but now they have seen and hated both me and my Father" (v. 24).

So the world hates us. As relational creatures, that truth can gnaw at us. We crave acceptance. We long to be loved. We desire to be esteemed, valued, and respected. We can yearn for those things from the world.

But Jesus says that acceptance will never happen. The world doesn't love us. The world doesn't even like us. The world *hates* us. Jesus tells us so we aren't surprised when persecution comes. Later, when John wrote his first epistle, he said, "Do not be surprised, brothers, that the world hates you" (1 John 3:13). As American believers, this can be an unexpected revelation. But it shouldn't be. The Bible is abundantly clear on this point.

WHY THE WORLD HATES US

Why does the world hate us? You may find it unfathomable. You're a nice person. You obey the laws, pay your taxes, volunteer at the local homeless shelter, recycle faithfully—you're the kind of person that has made America such a great country! Why does the world hate people like you and me? In John 15:19–24, Jesus gives us three reasons the world hates us.

We're Different

The first reason the world hates us is because we're different. "If you were of the world, the world would love you as its own; but because you are not of the world, but I chose you out of the world, therefore the world hates you" (v. 19).

I mentioned earlier that the Greek language has several kinds of conditional statements. The conditional statement in verse 19 is different from the one in verse 18. Whereas the first one assumed the reality of what was said, the one Jesus uses in verse 19 assumes the statement is *not* true. He is saying, "if you were of the world (and you are not), the world would love you because it loves its own."

This indicates the world loves some people. It shows love for those who identify with, conform to, and embrace its values. If we fit the worldly mold we would gain the world's love; it would love us because we would be one of them.

But if we don't conform to the world, the world holds zero tolerance for us. Instead of accepting us into the club, it rejects us. According to Jesus, that's the problem. We aren't like the world because He *chose* us out of the world.

In eternity past, Jesus elected us (Eph. 1:4). In time and space, He saved us. With salvation came a total transformation of our life's orientation. We have a different allegiance, value system, and destiny. John emphasizes this with his readers in 1 John 4:4–6 when he says, "Little children, you are from God . . . they are from the world; therefore they speak from the world and the world listens to them. We are from God."

> **THE WORLD doesn't love us. The world doesn't even like us.**

64

In short, John says there, "You are different. You are not of the world." Because that is true, the world resents us. It demands that we conform, and if we don't—due to our biblical convictions—we bear the world's wrath. D. A. Carson reflects on this:

> Raw secularism, greedy materialism, immoral special-interest groups seeking privilege or "alternative lifestyles" which are biblically indefensible, all with one accord resent the Christian who stands up and lovingly insists "Thus says the Lord."[1]

We Bear Christ's Name

The second reason the world hates us is because we bear Christ's name and identify with Him. Jesus says in John 15:20–21, "Remember the word that I said to you: 'A servant is not greater than his master.' If they persecuted me, they will also persecute you. If they kept my word, they will also keep yours. But all these things they will do to you on account of my name, because they do not know him who sent me."

In an interesting twist, Jesus quotes Himself. "A servant is not greater than his master," were words He said to His disciples earlier that night in the upper room as He humbly washed their feet (John 13:16).

In the original setting, Jesus used this phrase to teach and model servant leadership. When He repeats it in chapter 15, His application is different. In verse 20 He's teaching us that we shouldn't think we'll escape the treatment He receives. If the world persecuted Him (and they did), we can expect they'll persecute us. As the master, so the slave.

Jesus says this will assuredly happen because we bear the name of Christ. "All these things they will do to you on account of my name" (v. 21a).

This means the world doesn't hate us because of who we are. If we cut to the chase, we're nothing.

This means the world doesn't hate us because of what we've done. None of that is worth anything.

Instead, this means the world hates us because of the badge we wear. We've publicly and purposefully identified with Jesus Christ. They hate Him—so they hate us.

While it's not likely the disciples understood these words completely when they first heard them, they understood later. After the day of Pentecost and the coming of the Holy Spirit, the disciples recognized they were being punished for their identification with Christ. In Acts 5 they're flogged by the Sanhedrin for their preaching. After being released "they left the presence of the council, rejoicing that they were counted worthy to suffer dishonor for the name" (v. 41). They suffered because of His name. It will be the same for us.

In many ways, this doesn't make sense. We could expect to be hated if we identify with a serial killer such as Ted Bundy. Or we could expect hatred from the world if we identified with Adolf Hitler and the Nazi party. But Jesus? The one who healed people? The one who had compassion for them? The one who took five loaves and two fish and fed thousands of people? Why does our identification with Jesus bring hate? The third reason provides the answer.

We Expose Their Sin

The world hates us because Christ in us exposes their sin. Jesus said to His disciples, "If I had not come and spoken to them, they would not have been guilty of sin, but now they have no excuse for their sin. . . . If I had not done among them the works that no one else did, they would not be guilty of sin, but now they have seen and hated both me and my Father" (vv. 22, 24).

These words could be misunderstood. Note Jesus isn't saying man would be innocent or sinless if He hadn't come and spoke the

Word to them. That interpretation would ignore where Jesus says, "but now they have no excuse for their sin" (v. 22).

It means that by coming to earth, Jesus exposed the world's sin. The sin was always there. Romans 3:23 makes this clear: "For all have sinned and fall short of the glory of God." But with Christ's advent into the world, like light coming into darkness, sin was exposed.

Jesus explained this to Nicodemus in John 3, "And this is the judgment: the light has come into the world, and people loved the darkness rather than the light because their works were evil. For everyone who does wicked things hates the light and does not come to the light, lest his works should be exposed" (vv. 19–20). Notice two important things in this statement: (1) the world hates the light, and (2) the light (Jesus) exposes the wickedness of the world.

Jesus does the same thing—exposing sin—through His followers preaching His Word. When we teach what God says in His Word, the light of Christ shines on the sin of man and exposes it. Christ in us, taking the Word spoken through us, shines a floodlight on the world's evil. The deeds of darkness are revealed.

But the world hates that. They hate having their sin exposed, so they hate us. They hate us because we're different from them, we've identified with Christ, and Christ in us exposes their sin.

Therefore, when a new government regulation punishes you for your faith, or when an office policy seems to single you out for discipline because of your biblical values, or when your own family gives you the "cold shoulder" because you have not been silent about your Christian beliefs, take heart. You're not alone. The world hates Christ. And therefore, the world hates us.

AN EXTREME COMMITMENT

When we grasp the reality of the world's hate, we can better understand the context of Christ's commands in Matthew 16:24–

27—including the command to take up our cross. These are familiar words, but without an environment of persecution we often fail to understand the extreme commitment Jesus requires of His disciples.

The words come at a hinge point in Matthew's gospel. In chapters 1–15, Jesus demonstrates His identity as the Messiah of God through His words and works. After providing them one last demonstration in the feeding of the four thousand, Jesus moves His band of disciples north into Caesarea Philippi and asks them a pair of probing questions.

First He asks, "Who do people say that the Son of Man is?" (16:13). He receives a variety of responses. Then He asks, "Who do you say that I am?" which spurs Peter to give his famous confession, "You are the Christ, the Son of the living God" (v. 16). From this moment, Jesus knew they understood who He was. Now He would explain what He'd come to do and what that would require of them. Therefore, 16:24–27 begins Jesus' teaching on discipleship—what He requires of His followers.

The passage's structure is straightforward. In verse 24 Jesus lists three requirements for discipleship. Each requirement is linked to a different command. You could consider this a definition of discipleship. (In the next three verses, Jesus gives two reasons why each of us should make the extreme commitments to be His disciple, but for now I'll only discuss the requirements of discipleship.)

> **WHEN YOUR own family gives you the cold shoulder because of your Christian beliefs, take heart. You're not alone.**

"If anyone would come after me, let him deny himself, and take up his cross and follow me" (v. 24). Before listing the three requirements for discipleship, let me note two essential features of the call to discipleship.

DISCIPLESHIP IS OPEN TO ALL

First, the call is open to anyone. This is reaffirmed in verse 25 when Jesus says, "whoever." As there is a universal call in the gospel—whoever believes in Him should not perish but have eternal life (John 3:16)—there's also a universal call in discipleship. It is open to whoever, anyone, and everyone. If we believe in Christ, the call goes out to us. We're included in the "whoever."

DISCIPLESHIP IS AN ACT OF THE WILL

Second, this commitment is an act of the will. Jesus says, "If anyone would come after me," using a verb meaning "to wish" or "to desire." The word shows that there's volitional choice involved. We must make a thoughtful, prayerful, intentional decision to "come after" Christ. Therefore, while God sovereignly elects us unto salvation and irresistibly draws us to Himself (so all who are chosen come to faith), discipleship is a choice—an act of the will.

What does the commitment require? Read on.

Requirement 1: Renounce Self

The first requirement, tied to the first command, is to *renounce self*. "If anyone would come after me, let him deny himself." Jesus isn't calling us to become modern-day ascetics who deny themselves certain pleasures because they believe doing so gains them merit with God. Church history is filled with examples of ascetics, including one monk who lived on the top of a pole for years.

But asceticism isn't Jesus' intent when He calls us to deny ourselves. It's a call to renounce self. Grant Osborne comments, "To follow as God demands is to renounce the centrality of self."[2] Christ isn't asking us to necessarily give up creaturely comforts, but to renounce our life's self-interests—plentiful in affluent America. When we follow self, we pursue things that make us look good in others' eyes. We look for the lucrative career, the fancy titles, and the juicy perks. That's what self wants.

However, such self-interests inevitably conflict with a disciple's life. They'll place us at a fork in the road where we cannot do what self *and* God want. This conflict is why Jesus' requirement for disciples is to renounce self. He says give up the self-directed life. Toss away all the selfish conditions we put on serving Him, and instead make Christ the Master of our lives.

Requirement 2: Sacrifice Self

The second requirement of a disciple takes this commitment a step further: *be willing to sacrifice yourself* ("Take up his cross," v. 24).

Within the New Testament context of persecution, this command provides a powerful metaphor. Everyone in the Roman Empire knew the cross as an instrument of torture, designed to put someone to death. The condemned person would carry the crosspiece to the execution site where he would be brutally nailed to the wood and left to die. Osborne writes, "The disciples had to know, with all the opposition to Jesus by the officials, that this was a real possibility for them."[3]

Unfortunately, in our Western setting we typically empty this command of its intended commitment. Without the reality of persecution, we trivialize cross-bearing and identify it with any form of discomfort. But the cross is not ordinary human troubles or sorrows. It's not experiencing disease, poverty, or loss. The cross represents the ultimate sacrifice. To "take up our cross" means a commitment to die, if the Master requires it.

Each of the disciples surrounding Jesus (except the betrayer, Judas) took up their cross. Ten of them died a martyr's death. The other, John, died in exile. Penner comments, "Is it any wonder that the early church turned their world upside down? They were ready to sacrifice anything to get the message of Jesus Christ to a world for which their Lord died."[4]

Church history is filled with examples of others who picked up their crosses. In Oxford, England, there is a majestic statue commemorating three reformers who died for Christ: Hugh Latimer, Nicholas Ridley, and Thomas Cranmer. Cranmer, the Archbishop of Canterbury, was forced to watch Latimer and Ridley be burned at the stake on October 16, 1555. As the fires were being lit, Latimer cried out to Ridley, "Be of good comfort, Master Ridley, and play the man. We shall this day light such a candle by God's grace in England as I trust will never be put out."

His friend's courage impressed Cranmer, but his fear of likewise being burned at the stake led him to sign a bill of recantation, which effectively saved his life but denied his Christ. It's as if he said, "Enough's enough. I'm putting my cross down." Later he became so distraught by what he'd done that he went to the officials and publicly recanted his recantation. When he was led to the stake he held out his hand and asked that it be burned first, for it was the hand that signed the bill of recantation. He suffered martyrdom on March 21, 1556.

> **WITHOUT THE reality of persecution, we trivialize cross-bearing and identify it with any form of discomfort.**

Cross-bearing isn't just for saints of the past. It's also for saints in the present. Every day Jesus' followers around this world are asked to pay the ultimate price for their faith. With persecution coming to America, we need to know cross-bearing is a requirement for Christ's disciples. While the Master may not require death from each of us— or any of us—we must be *willing* to sacrifice ourselves.

Requirement 3: Keep Following Jesus

The last requirement for Jesus' disciples is tied to the final imperative verb in John 16:24. A disciple must *keep following Jesus*. He says, "Let him deny himself, take up his cross and *follow* me" (emphasis mine).

Jesus intentionally changes verb tenses with this final command. This verb, unlike the previous two, is in the present tense and has a continuative sense. It means we are to follow Jesus, and keep following Jesus, and never stop following Jesus. It means we cannot renounce self just once or take up our cross once and consider it sufficient. Instead, the discipleship Christ requires is a "day to day to day" following that never stops.

Therefore, a disciple of Jesus keeps following Him despite pain, or opposition, or persecution, or the threat of death. "The third command . . . stresses a life of continuous discipleship. Until the kingdom reality outweighs every consideration, even one's own life, one is not a true follower."[5]

"SHARE IN SUFFERING"

With the clear testimony of Scripture, we shouldn't be surprised when we experience persecution in America. We know the world hates us. We know discipleship requires us to unflinchingly renounce self-interest, commit to being sacrificed (if necessary), and keep following Jesus. But, despite that, we can still be surprised when we encounter enemies.

To that end, two clarifying passages—one from Paul and one from Peter—are instructive. As Paul neared his execution he wrote a final letter to his beloved protégé Timothy. Not naturally courageous, Timothy tended to shrink from conflict (as may be true for us). Paul calls him to "not be ashamed of the testimony about our Lord, nor of me his prisoner, but share in suffering for the gospel by the power of God" (2 Tim. 1:8). Paul repeated the call when he wrote, "Share in suffering as a good soldier of Christ Jesus" (2:3).

Knowing his young disciple well, Paul realized Timothy still might want to lag back from the front lines of the spiritual battle if such meant hardship and suffering. So in chapter 3, Paul recounts suffering he endured during his ministry. He speaks of "my persecutions and sufferings that happened to me at Antioch, at Iconium, and at Lystra—which persecutions I endured; yet from them all the Lord rescued me" (v. 11). As a resident of Lystra, Timothy would have been well aware of the hostility Paul faced there.

But Paul wasn't finished. After reviewing his sufferings, he continues in verse 12 to tell Timothy, "Indeed, all who desire to live a godly life in Christ Jesus will be persecuted." Timothy couldn't avoid these implications, and neither can we. Do we desire to live a godly life in Christ Jesus? If we want to display godliness as a fully devoted disciple of Christ, Paul says to be prepared. All who desire to follow Jesus will be persecuted. Suffering isn't just the lot of esteemed church leaders; it's an anticipated experience for every believer. The form of the persecution may vary from country to country and from age to age, but the world's hatred of believers remains unchanged.

A DISCIPLE of Jesus keeps following Him despite pain, or opposition, or persecution, or even the threat of death.

Peter gives a similar message in 1 Peter 4. In later chapters I'll discuss the rich material appearing in this epistle. For now I only want to note the perspective he shares with his suffering readers in verse 12: "Beloved, do not be surprised at the fiery trial when it comes upon you to test you, as though something strange were happening to you." The verbal construction Peter uses combined with the negative carries the force of a prohibition. It implies his readers were bewildered at the hostility they were facing, and Peter calls them to stop being shocked. Persecution is not something strange or foreign to the Christian life—even though it's unpleasant. As much as we might wish it otherwise, persecution is normal.

THE NEW NORMAL

As American believers—novices to suffering—this first counterintuitive principle that persecution is *normal, not strange* is most important. For reasons only known in the eternal mind of God, we've escaped persecution for the first two centuries of our nation's existence. This freedom allowed the American church to flourish and take the lead in evangelizing other parts of the world. From our limited perspective, this seems not only normal, but preferable.

Not true. What's normal in the Christian life, starting with the first believers in the fledgling church in Jerusalem and continuing today in the global church, is persecution. Once we accept that and don't chafe against it, we'll realize the spiritual benefits that make suffering preferable. I will explore the blessings gained through persecution in the next chapter.

4

BLESSED NOT CURSED

Blessed are you when others revile you and
persecute you and utter all kinds of evil
against you falsely on my account.

MATTHEW 5:11

It's Sunday morning. You get to church a few minutes early and grab a cup of coffee at the gourmet bar in the lobby. As you are stirring in creamer, you see your friend Matt enter. You wave, he comes over, and you engage in the normal pleasantries marking a conversation at church.

As you catch up on the latest in Matt's life, you learn that he and his wife just bought their dream house in an upscale neighborhood. Matt's significant promotion at work—with a sizeable raise—made the purchase possible. Your conversation ends, and you shift toward the worship service. Matt acknowledges, "We feel really blessed."

You've had this type of conversation before. So have I—hundreds of times. It occurs weekly, even daily, between Christians across America and shows the curious spin we put on the word *blessing*.

We equate blessing with a new job, a new house, a banner year for our company, a big bonus at work, a new baby, a clean medical report, or an acceptance into the college of our choice. In our Western mindset—conditioned by the affluence surrounding us—God's blessings are pleasant and enjoyable.

When the opposite happens—suffering, hardship, loss of job, loss of health, financial strain—"blessing" isn't usually the first word off our lips. As we cope with trials, we wonder if we're being punished by God. We question if we've somehow merited God's judgment. And we fervently pray that the burdens will be removed.

In God's economy, blessings are radically different than our American perception. This is the second counterintuitive principle we learn from Scripture: *persecution means you're blessed, not cursed.*

THE MEANING OF "BLESSED"

While we may wrestle with the concept of persecution representing blessing, God doesn't stutter on this topic. Four times the New Testament declares this truth. In the Sermon on the Mount, Jesus states it twice. "Blessed are those who are persecuted for righteousness' sake, for theirs is the kingdom of heaven" (Matt. 5:10). In the very next verse He says, "Blessed are you when others revile you and persecute you and utter all kinds of evil against you falsely on my account" (v. 11).

In his first epistle, Peter encourages suffering readers saying, "But even if you should suffer for righteousness' sake, you will be blessed" (3:14). Finally, James teaches the same truth to his flock in James 1:12: "Blessed is the man who remains steadfast under trial."

These verses challenge our American mindset, conditioned to think divine blessings are always pleasant. Paul, Peter, and James challenge us to understand what the Bible means by *blessed*, and how persecution brings blessing.

Our confusion about the meaning of *blessed* is partly because of the different ways Bible versions translate this word. Some say "blessed," others say "happy," and still other say "fortunate." All hold a measure of truth.

The Greek word is *makarios.* For Greeks, *makarios* involved the happy contentment which came from self-containment. If you were *makarios,* you had all the material blessings and physical possessions you needed to exist without worry. In secular Greek usage the island of Cyprus is called "the *makarios* isle" or "the blest isle." Cyprus gained this title because its inhabitants never had to leave its shores to have everything they needed to be content. They had natural resources, minerals, lush vegetation and fruit—they had it all. The island was self-contained; no Cypriot had to search outside for the needs and wants of life.

This idea carries over into the biblical text with one major modification: when God blesses you, He's giving His stamp of approval. God never blesses anyone or anything He doesn't approve of. So when you experience God's hand of blessing, you can be confident He approves of who you are, what you are, and what you're doing. That knowledge brings the happiness of contentment.

PAUL: GAIN AND LOSS

However, we may wonder: how does persecution bring blessing? We understand how an unexpected financial windfall or unanticipated promotion represents blessing. But persecution and suffering—not so much. So how does persecution allow us to experience the inner contentment that comes from knowing we stand approved before God?

The New Testament gives us two ways persecution brings blessing.

PERSECUTION ALLOWS US TO KNOW CHRIST MORE

The apostle Paul was well acquainted with persecution. In writing to the Corinthian church, which—much like us—placed a high value on comfort and ease, he gave a short but graphic list of his sufferings:

> Five times I received at the hands of Jews the forty lashes less one. Three times I was beaten with rods. Once I was stoned. Three times I was shipwrecked; a night and a day I was adrift at sea; on frequent journeys, in danger from rivers, danger from robbers, danger from my own people, danger from Gentiles, danger in the city, danger in the wilderness, danger at sea, danger from false brothers, in toil and hardship, through many a sleepless night, in hunger and thirst, often without food, in cold and exposure. (2 Cor. 11:24–27)

Undoubtedly, Paul knew suffering. As he writes the book of Philippians, the apostle is enduring one of those many sufferings—he's imprisoned in Rome awaiting trial before Caesar. In chapter three, Paul explains to us how suffering allows us to become more intimate with Christ. He tells us how persecution can enable us to know our Savior better.

GOD NEVER blesses anyone or anything He doesn't approve of.

Philippians 3:4–10 reads like an accounting ledger. In verses 4 through 6 Paul talks about what's considered gain. In verses 7–8 he explains why he considered all that as loss, and in 9–10 he shares why this transaction was necessary.

PAUL'S GAIN

Paul had an impressive resume. "If anyone else thinks he has reason for confidence in the flesh, I have more: circumcised on the eighth day, of the people of Israel, of the tribe of Benjamin, a Hebrew of Hebrews; as to the law, a Pharisee; as to zeal, a persecutor of the church; as to righteousness under the law, blameless" (Philippians 3:4–6).

In ancient Israel, this was a flawless pedigree. Paul lists five things, both inherited advantages and personal achievements, which distinguished him from most of his contemporaries.

1. His rite: the rite of circumcision.

"I was circumcised on the eighth day" (v. 5a). Circumcision placed him in Abraham's covenant community. Mosaic Law required a male child to be circumcised on the eighth day after birth as a physical sign of this covenant. Paul says, "I have that. Check."

2. His race: a member of the Hebrew nation.

"I am a member of the nation of Israel, the tribe of Benjamin, a Hebrew of Hebrews" (v. 5b). Paul was born a member of God's covenant people. He wasn't a proselyte—an outsider who saw the truth and joined the club. He was a pure-blooded Israelite and member of God's people. Check.

3. His religion: a Pharisee.

"As to the law, a Pharisee" (v. 5c). Few joined this exclusive fraternity. The historian Josephus said there were only about six thousand Pharisees in Israel. There were few because the vow required more—not only diligently keeping the Law of Moses, but also following the hundreds of laws the Pharisees believed kept them pure. Paul says, "I was not only a Jew, I was a Pharisee. Check."

4. His reputation: zealous.

"As to zeal, a persecutor of the church" (v. 6a). The book of Acts records this for us. It shows Paul was not just a Pharisee, but a Pharisee terrorist. In his zeal for his traditions, he sought to obliterate those of The Way. He hunted them down and took pleasure in killing them. Zeal? Check.

5. His righteousness: blameless.

"As to righteousness under the law, found blameless" (v. 6b). Notice Paul doesn't say he's sinless before God. He specifically says that according to the righteousness found in the Law—which meant the meticulous observance of 613 commandments developed in Judaism—he was blameless. "I did it all. I kept it all. Check and check."

This is an impressive list of accomplishments. In that day and culture those credentials would put him on the top of the heap. Born right. Bred well. Accomplished much. You want gain? You want prestige? Paul had it. If Israelite pop culture included celebrity magazines such as *People* and *Us*, Paul would've regularly graced their covers.

But he's not alone in his pedigree-building pursuits. We all possess gain. Some is inherited—a distinguished family legacy. Some is achieved—advanced degrees from prestigious institutions. Some is bestowed—impressive titles and positions. We may not match Paul's impeccable resume, but we all have gain. It's the stuff that appears in your obituary when you die.

Gain is not sinful. Being born into a privileged family isn't sin. Achieving high levels of education isn't wrong. Accomplishing much in your profession isn't bad. It's gain. Some have more or less, but we all have some.

PAUL'S LOSS

However, once we come to saving faith in Christ, we need to view gain as loss. "But whatever gain I had, I counted as loss for the sake of Christ" (v. 7). When Paul talks about gain and loss here, he uses an accounting word. It speaks of recording something in a ledger. Paul is saying, "I used to count all these things in my past on the positive side of the ledger. They were gain to me. But no more. Now I record them on the negative side of the ledger. Now I consider them to be loss."

This doesn't mean Paul lost all those things. Some he did lose, some he didn't. But he counted, considered, and valued them differently. Once they were important; now they weren't. Once they were valuable; now they weren't. Once they were gain; now they were loss.

This is a strong statement. Notice Paul emphasizes it by repeating the thought twice in verse 8 expanding and intensifying it each time. "Indeed, I count everything as loss because of the surpassing worth of knowing Christ Jesus my Lord" (v. 8a).

This part of the verse expands his thought. Initially he said the things that were gain were now considered loss. Now he says he counts everything as loss. This refers to things he didn't list before, such as his Roman citizenship, material possessions, and training under Gamaliel. Everything—all of it—was now considered loss.

In the second half of verse 8, Paul intensifies his point even more. "For his sake I have suffered the loss of all things and count them as rubbish" (v. 8b).

Translations differ for *rubbish*. Some render it "refuse"; others translate it as "dung." The word here is *skubala*, and it's borderline vulgar. Only used this one time in the New Testament, it's commonly used to refer to human excrement or the foul-smelling filth thrown into the streets for dogs. It's not a pretty word. But it's what Paul uses to describe his powerful and visceral feelings. "All of this is not just loss to me, it's—it's dung!" It wasn't just negative. It was repulsive.

"THE SURPASSING WORTH"

Why did Paul feel so strongly about this? Why did he consider all the gain to be not just loss, but repulsive? Wasn't he grateful?

Didn't he appreciate who he was and what he'd accomplished? Didn't he value that he was a Jew and a member of God's covenant people?

Paul wasn't ungrateful, but his radical change of perspective came because he valued something else more: knowing Christ fully. "Indeed, I count everything as loss because of the surpassing worth of knowing Christ Jesus my Lord" (v. 8).

Here Paul makes a comparative statement. He acknowledges that all the things from his past had value. But he says *this* has much more value. Compared to *this*, all of that is just dung. What is *this*? "Knowing Christ Jesus my Lord."

Please don't overlook that Paul calls Christ "*my* Lord." This is noteworthy because it's the only time he refers to Christ this way. It adds further depth of feeling. Paul says, "All of that in my past I count as loss because of the surpassing worth of knowing Christ Jesus *my* Lord."

Such knowledge of Christ isn't just intellectual, like you might have of math or physics. Instead the word used indicates an experiential knowledge of someone. This is the knowledge you have of a husband, a wife, a child, or a grandchild. This knowledge isn't static; it's always growing and developing, deepening and becoming more intimate. Paul first met Christ personally on the Damascus road in Acts 9. Now, here in Philippians 3 he says, "I want to know Him fully. I want to know Him completely. I want to know Him intimately. I want to *know* Him."

Knowing Christ is the highest ambition in life. Jeremiah 9:23–24 states, "Let not the wise man boast in his wisdom, let not the mighty man boast in his might, let not the rich man boast in his riches, but let him who boasts, boast in this, that he understands and knows me."

You can give yourself to this pursuit and you will never exhaust Him. You can plunge to the depths of His being and you'll always find He runs deeper. There's always more to know, to love, and to understand.

But to get there—and this is key—you must consider everything else to be loss. All of it. All the gain, all the stuff, all the advantages, all the privileges. All of it is loss. All of it is dung.

HOW "LOSS" MEANS GAIN

You might be disconnecting at the moment. You might be asking, "Why is it necessary to count all things as loss in order to know Christ better and better?" Here's why: because the gain can inhibit us from knowing Christ better. Paul explains this in the final two verses of the Philippians 3 passage. In verses 9 and 10 Paul shows what it means to know Christ through two explanatory statements. The first is positional in nature (representing our spiritual position in Christ), the second is practical.

SHARE IN HIS RIGHTEOUSNESS

First—positionally—Paul says knowing Christ means *sharing in His righteousness.* "(That I may gain Christ) and be found in him, not having a righteousness of my own that comes from the law, but that which comes through faith in Christ, the righteousness from God that depends on faith" (v. 9).

You don't gain this positional righteousness through your own merits. Paul tried that. This righteousness "comes through faith in Christ." This is justification. This is what Paul talked about in Romans 4 when he said, "For what does the Scripture say? 'Abraham believed God, and it was counted to him as righteousness.' Now to the one who works, his wages are not counted as a gift, but as his due. And to the one who does not work but believes in him who justifies the ungodly, his faith is counted as righteousness" (vv. 3–5).

This is a knowledge of Christ, but it is positional and initial. Paul gained this knowledge when he met Jesus on the Damascus road. But he wanted more. He wanted not just an initial knowledge of Christ, but an intimate knowledge of Christ; therefore, he provides a second explanation of knowing Christ in verse 10. "That I may know him and the power of his resurrection, and may share his sufferings, becoming like him in his death."

SHARE IN HIS SUFFERING

Paul's first experience of knowing Christ was positional and initial. His second was practical and intimate. To know Christ is to know "the power of his resurrection and . . . share in his sufferings." This means to know Christ intimately requires us to *share in His sufferings*. Suffering is required because that is who He is. He is the suffering servant. He is the Man of Sorrows. Over 2700 years ago, Isaiah described Him:

He was despised and rejected by men; a man of sorrows, and acquainted with grief; and as one from whom men hide their faces; he was despised and we esteemed him not. Surely he has borne our griefs and carried our sorrows; yet we esteemed him stricken, smitten by God, and afflicted. But he was pierced for our transgressions; he was crushed for our iniquities; upon him was the chastisement that brought us peace, and with his wounds we are healed. (Isaiah 53:3–5)

This is who Christ is. This is what Christ did. He suffered.

Therefore, if we want to know Him intimately, Paul says we have to "share in his sufferings." The word *share* is the common Greek word *koinonia*, meaning "to participate or share together in." This is God's design for His children. We share in His sufferings. As we suffer, we'll know "the power of his resurrection." We'll experience His strength. We'll understand what it means to be carried along in difficult circumstances in ways we cannot explain or comprehend. As we suffer, we'll know Him more and more.

WHAT HOLDS US BACK

What's keeping us from intimate knowledge of Christ? What's preventing us from sharing in His sufferings and knowing Him better? Our gain in life, i.e., the advantages and privileges we enjoy. This gain prevents us from knowing Christ better because we don't want to give it all up through suffering. Sharing in Christ's sufferings normally means gains get sacrificed. We lose our status. We forfeit our possessions. We sacrifice our reputation.

Paul lost his gains. He went from being viewed as one of the rising stars in Jerusalem to a hated man with a price on his head. He went from enjoying the pride of being a Pharisee to the humility and indignity of escaping his enemies via a basket lowered over a wall. He went from being the arrestor of Christians to the one arrested. He was beaten, derided, and died mostly forsaken through a grisly execution in a Roman prison.

But something wonderful happened through this process. Through suffering, Paul came to know Jesus his Lord better. He became intimate with his Savior by learning what it meant to share in Christ's sufferings.

This is a blessing! But it's a blessing we'll never experience unless we're willing to sacrifice our gain, suffer loss, and expose ourselves to persecution. Therefore, we each need to ask ourselves, "What am I unwilling to surrender? What am I hesitant to sacrifice in my identification with Christ? What am I reluctant to lose? My status in the community? My financial future? My title and education? My home and possessions?"

It's important to identify what's holding us back from willingness to suffer, because that is what is also holding us back from a more intimate knowledge of Christ. Until we're willing to count it all as dung and suffer its loss, we cannot know intimately the One who was the suffering servant.

Ultimately, God may not require that we suffer the loss of all things; He has different plans for each of us. But whether He requires that of us isn't going to matter, because we've already decided it's all dung. We've decided the most important thing in our life is knowing Christ.

Persecution brings blessing because it allows us to know Christ more. But there is also a second way persecution brings blessing.

PERSECUTION ALLOWS US TO BECOME MORE LIKE CHRIST

This principle appears in the first chapter of the epistle of James. The compassionate shepherd wrote to a dispersed and harassed flock, "Count it all joy, my brothers, when you meet trials of various kinds, for you know that the testing of your faith produces steadfastness. And let steadfastness have its full effect, that you may be perfect and complete, lacking in nothing" (vv. 2–4).

James's readers knew about persecution. The epistle's backdrop is the first nine chapters of Acts. The church is still largely Jewish, but the sharp persecution in Jerusalem spawned by Stephen's death in Acts 7 and 8 caused many of the Jewish believers to flee for safety in other cities. They had hoped their new locations would ease their suffering. For the most part, it didn't.

Back in Jerusalem. James is concerned for them and encourages them as they seek to live by faith in their hostile communities. He doesn't mince words when he says, "Count it all joy, my brothers, when you meet trials of various kinds" (v. 2).

When this passage is preached in American churches we identify the trials with various challenges we might face in life such as medical issues, family conflict, unemployment, or sudden tragedy. While this isn't an invalid interpretation, these difficulties are profoundly different from the trials James's readers experienced. Their trials weren't the garden variety.

The word for *trials—peirasmoi—*along with the attached verb, implies "the reference is not to minor little irritations, but to larger adverse experiences which cannot be avoided."[1] Dan McCartney writes, "The context makes clear that James is thinking of the various pressures often applied against believers that threaten their well-being, which may very well cause believers to doubt the sovereignty of God in their lives."[2] Therefore, the "trials of various kinds" were the diverse ways in which they were facing persecution in their lives.

COUNTING IT JOY

When (not if) such persecution arises, James calls us to face it in what appears to be an irrational way. He says "count it all joy" (v. 2). The verb used means we are to make a deliberate, conscious, and careful decision to experience joy even in the midst of suffering. We are not to complain, shrink back, or express despair. Instead we are to greet suffering with joy.

The obvious question is, "Why? Why would God want His children to face suffering and trials with joy? Why does He want them to make this deliberate choice?" James offers a two-part answer.

SUFFERING PRODUCES SPIRITUAL FORTITUDE

First, we are to greet trials with joy because of suffering's immediate effect: the development of spiritual fortitude. "For you know that the testing of your faith produces steadfastness" (v. 3). The word for *steadfastness* is common in the New Testament and carries the idea of staying under a heavy load instead of seeking to escape.

Edmond Hiebert writes, "It is not a passive attitude of quiet submission or resignation, but rather, a brave manliness which confronts the difficulties and contends against them."[3]

This ability to "keep on keeping on," even when we are experiencing pain and difficulties, is a highly desirable virtue. It's the ability to stay the course and not jettison the hardship despite the suffering. Unfortunately, it's a trait that cannot be realized without suffering.

We need suffering to develop spiritual fortitude. It's the chrysalis principle: if you free a butterfly from its chrysalis when it's struggling to liberate itself, you'll destroy it. The butterfly won't develop the strength it needs to soar with its big, beautiful wings; it'll be condemned to a weak, inept quality of life.

In a similar way, if we lack spiritual fortitude, there's a reason. We haven't been toughened by suffering and trials. We've had a soft life. We've jumped from underneath the trials that appeared and never developed spiritual fortitude.

Clearly, American Christians have had it easy. We've not faced persecution on a regular basis like our brothers and sisters around the world. But that's about to change. A hostile culture is bringing persecution our way. The first reason we should greet such suffering with joy is because, if we stay under the trials, they will create priceless spiritual fortitude in our lives.

But there is also a second reason we should greet trials with joy.

SUFFERING PERFECTS OUR CHARACTER

James tells us to face trials with joy because they produce spiritual fortitude. Then he continues to explain spiritual fortitude has a purpose—perfecting our character. "And let steadfastness have its full effect, that you may be perfect and complete, lacking in nothing" (v. 4).

Don't overlook the three-letter word standing second in that sentence: *let*. James says, "*Let* steadfastness have its full effect." There's more to character development than trials. Suffering doesn't produce spiritual maturity by default. If it is repelled and not welcomed, suffering can be destructive and lead to bitterness.

But that doesn't have to be the case. Through persecution God provides us with a tool to powerfully sharpen our character by (1) letting steadfastness have its full effect, and (2) staying patiently under the trials, refusing to give up or get out.

When we do this, "steadfastness will have its full effect." We will find our character being developed so we are "perfect and complete, lacking in nothing." A literal rendering of that last phrase would be, "complete in all its parts, entire, or fully intact." It means everything needed is present; nothing more is required.

Have you ever sat down to play a board game with your family and discovered pieces were missing? Maybe the dice or the timer—or a piece that makes the whole game work? Because our family has had eleven home addresses through the years, we've had the opportunity to lose plenty of game pieces. The only way the game becomes useful is when you add in the needed pieces. You "perfect" or "complete" the game so it's "lacking in nothing."

Since we're sinners saved by grace, when we come to faith in Christ each of us has plenty of pieces of our character missing. We each have thousands of character points to be added or refined. God's encouraging truth says He has ways He accomplishes that work in our lives. One way—a key way—is through trials. When they come, if we stay under the trials—not dodging a painful situation or seeking an easy exit but pursuing the maximum spiritual benefit they offer—God uses them in the perfecting process. A rough edge of our character softens. A missing virtue is added. Slowly but surely, God's perfecting work takes shape in our lives.

Who will we resemble? Christ. A character "perfect and complete, lacking in nothing" is Christlike. While we'll never arrive at perfection in this life, it makes for an exciting journey. And it gives us every reason to greet trials with joy.

THE BLESSING WE'VE MISSED

In God's economy, persecution means *we're blessed, not cursed.* Persecution brings blessing because it allows us to know Christ more. Persecution brings blessing because it allows us to become more like Christ.

For years we've sung *God Bless America,* and we've usually associated divine blessing with prosperity and freedom. Certainly that's blessing because every good gift and all freedom comes from God. But there's a significant part of God's blessing we missed in America —the blessing that comes with persecution.

Perhaps the cultural change in our country and the arrival of persecution for believers is God's answer to our plea, "God bless America!" Perhaps believers in America will be able to experience divine blessing like never before in our history. Believers in the rest of the world know and experience this blessing. Maybe it's time for us to get in on the party.

5

EXPOSED NOT PROTECTED

Behold, I am sending you out as sheep
in the midst of wolves, so be wise
as serpents and innocent as doves.

———

MATTHEW 10:16

Imagine a girl on a school playground. She's small and shy, but participating with the others playing tag and jump rope. She laughs with her friends—until an older, stocky boy begins harassing her.

He sneers as he belittles her, calling her nasty names; she cowers. Emboldened by her response, he steps up the attack, shoving her until she stumbles into an isolated corner of the playground. She's frightened; in self-defense she turns her face away. The boy isn't satisfied and begins mercilessly punching her with meaty fists, his eyes glowing in hatred.

The girl's whimpers turn into gut-wrenching sobs. In between blows her eyes dart to the watching crowd, silently pleading with them to rescue her. The boy sees no one willing to defend her, so the senseless beating continues.

As she suffers, the girl wonders if her teacher will save her. What about her older brother—will he come to her rescue? She expects someone to help her. But no one does.

When we suffer unjustly, we expect others to defend us. As we prepare for persecution from a hostile culture, we expect to be lovingly supported by family members and ably defended by our government. But the third counterintuitive biblical principle is that *believers can expect to be exposed not protected.* This may not be true in every case, but as a general principle we shouldn't rely on family or government to defend us when persecution comes. Often they won't.

GOD'S ROLE FOR GOVERNMENT

Government was instituted by God, not man. The New Testament shows the role of government in two central passages: Romans 13:1–7 and 1 Peter 2:13–14. God placed this instruction in our Bibles, as Wayne Grudem says, "Not only to inform Christians about how they should relate to civil government, but also in order that people with governmental responsibilities could know what God himself expects from them."[1]

The longer passage, Romans 13, provides us with four principles about government.

1. Government Rulers Are Appointed by God

Paul writes, "For there is no authority except from God, and those that exist have been instituted by God" (v. 1). God's the source of all authority, and if any human authority exists—whether local, state, or federal—it receives authority from Him. This given authority isn't absolute, but delegated. The verb *exist* (*tasso*) means "to cause to stand" and is in the perfect tense. This means all authorities have been caused to stand by God, and they currently stand in that state of divine sanction.

Jesus explained this to Pilate at the trial when He said, "You would have no authority over me at all unless it had been given you from above" (John 19:11). In Romans 13:1 Paul does not allow for exceptions to this truth. He plainly says, "There *is no* authority except from God," which means this is as true for an oppressive dictatorship as it is for a Western democracy. All authority is sourced in God, no matter how they gained that authority or how well they administer it. As the

> **WHEN WE suffer unjustly, we expect others to defend us.**

sovereign Lord, God can remove leaders if He desires, as He proved often in Scripture. The prophet Daniel, in interpreting a dream of King Nebuchadnezzar, explained, "The Most High rules the kingdom of men and gives it to whom he will and sets over it the lowliest of men" (Dan. 4:17). A year later, in fulfillment of the dream, God humbled Nebuchadnezzar and relegated him to life with oxen for seven years.

2. Governmental Rulers Exist to Punish Evildoers

"Therefore, whoever resists the authorities resists what God has appointed, and those who resist will incur judgment. For rulers are not a terror to good conduct, but to bad" (13:2–3). As God's authority, the government has been given the responsibility to restrain evil. Rulers are to be a terror for wrongdoers, who know they run the risk of punishment if they persist in their evil. Later Paul says, "If you do wrong, be afraid, for he does not bear the sword in vain. For he is the servant of God, an avenger who carries out God's wrath on the wrongdoer" (v. 4). This implies governmental punishment is inflicted upon the evildoer.

As Grudem says, "The purpose of civil punishment is not only to prevent further wrongdoing, but also to carry out God's wrath on wrongdoing, and that this will include bringing actual punishment—that is, some kind of pain or hardship to the wrongdoer, a punishment that is appropriate to the crime committed."[2]

This assumes the government's laws reflect the moral code of

God's Word. If so, the wrath evildoers experience is the wrath of God for their sin. This infliction of punishment is the role of government, not individual citizens. "The vengeance that is prohibited to individual Christians (12:19) is executed by God's chosen servants, the secular authorities."[3] If we're wronged, we can't take matters into our own hands, but look to our government to bring justice.

3. Governmental Rulers Exist to Reward Those Who Do Good

"Would you have no fear of the one who is in authority? Then do what is good, and you will receive his approval" (13:3). The concern for government is for good, which refers to the inherent good citizens do in promoting a peaceable, quiet life beneficial to all (1 Tim. 2:2). Leon Morris says, "The ruler is God's servant to enable God's other servants to get on with the job of doing God's will."[4]

Good behavior can anticipate praise and approval from the government consistent with its desires to carry out its delegated duties from God. Grudem sums up: "These verses indicate that government has a role in promoting the common good of a society. It should not only punish wrongdoing but also encourage and reward good conduct, conduct that contributes to the good of society."[5]

4. Governmental Rulers Are Servants of God

Consistent with the theology of previous verses, Paul writes in verse 4 that a ruler is "God's servant for your good." He repeats himself: "the authorities are ministers of God" (v. 6).

The word *servant* (*diakonos*) is the same word used elsewhere to speak of Christian servants and ministers. It implies governments serve God whether they acknowledge it or not. Isaiah called Cyrus a servant of God (Isa. 45:1), as was Nebuchadnezzar (Jer. 25:9). Being God's servant renders a strong measure of accountability for anyone serving as a governmental leader. They cannot rule as they wish without one day giving account to God. Morris says, "The Emperor on his throne, and for that matter any petty local bureaucrat, might well see his power as something to be exercised as he chose. But Paul is clear that everyone in any position of responsibility is first and foremost God's servant and that it is to God that he will one day be forced to render account."[6]

The parallel passage to Romans 13—1 Peter 2:13–14—presents a consistent view of the role of government. Peter writes, "Be subject for the Lord's sake to every human institution, whether it be to the emperor as supreme, or to governors as sent by him to punish those who do evil and to praise those who do good." As Paul did, Peter explains that government is to serve God by rewarding those who do good and punishing those who do wrong.

GOVERNMENT IN A FALLEN WORLD

These biblical passages would seem to suggest we can expect our government to protect us from unjust persecution. If the government is God's servant, and it has the divine role of rewarding good and punishing evil, it seems a reasonable expectation. Unfortunately, government in a fallen world and facilitated by godless rulers often fails to fulfill its divine purpose. It doesn't always protect the righteous—but can (and does) persecute them.

A classic Old Testament example is in Daniel 6. The Medes and the Persians have replaced Babylon's government, and Darius is ruler over the province. Daniel, although elderly, is still faithfully serving in the newly organized government. Because of his impeccable character, he's elevated to a high position. Darius initially makes Daniel one of three officials with jurisdiction over the province (v. 2) but, thanks to Daniel's excellent spirit, the king places him in the top role (v. 3). Daniel is the model public servant, and the government appears to be fulfilling its role of "rewarding those who do good."

However, others in the Medo-Persian government were not

thrilled with the prospect of reporting to a Jewish refugee. They first seek to incriminate Daniel by finding ways he'd violated existing Persian law (v. 4a). Undoubtedly they expected to discover bribery or corruption in Daniel's past which allowed him to climb to his present perch in the empire. Perhaps they expected this because they'd used the same strategy to gain their own promotions.

Despite meticulous research, their dirt filters returned clean. The Bible proclaims that "they could find no ground for complaint or any fault, because he was faithful, and no error or fault was found in him" (v. 4b).

Stop and let those words sink in. Daniel had been in public service for more than sixty years. In any realm of government, especially a pagan empire, such a long tenure provides plenty of opportunity for compromise. I write these words in Chicago, Illinois, a city infamous for political corruption. If an audit were made of top officials today, it's likely none would have Daniel's record. His enemies searched for any shred of malfeasance, but Daniel was the model of integrity and faithfulness. No negligence, corruption, bribery, or shortcomings. The man was clean!

Frustrated in their inability to prosecute Daniel under existing law, his antagonists cleverly decide to create a new law. They wield their powerful influence with the king and succeed in snagging his signature on a new ordinance: "Whoever makes petition to any god or man for thirty days, except to you, O king, shall be cast into the den of lions" (v. 7).

Note the sequence. While Daniel is blameless under current law and has been an exemplary citizen and servant for his entire life, it doesn't exempt him from intentional persecution. They create a new law rendering righteousness illegal. The trap works and Daniel is arrested, sentenced, and dumped into the den of lions—despite the king's best efforts to save him. You know the story. Daniel has a slumber party with the lions but emerges unscathed (vv. 19–22).

My point? We shouldn't necessarily expect government to protect us from persecution. When Jesus returns and reigns in His prophesied kingdom, there'll be justice and righteousness for all (Isa. 11:2–5). Until then, despite a Constitution that appears to protect religious freedom, we shouldn't expect our government to protect us.

As Daniel 6 shows us, opponents to righteousness can modify or add to the law. We might be blameless, but while we live in a fallen world where civil rulers often don't fulfill God's purposes for government, we cannot depend upon them to protect us.

This doesn't mean we abdicate involvement in the political process. In a land providing a democratic process, we have the responsibility to engage. We don't abdicate, but we recognize that the government isn't our savior. We realize the core issue is spiritual, not political.

Erwin Lutzer writes, "At root we must remember that our battle in America at the most basic level is spiritual, not political or even moral. Thus, although we use all the opportunities at our disposal to stand against the trends of our culture, we might still just be throwing inkwells at the devil."[7]

Jesus warned His disciples they would be forced to defend themselves before governmental authorities. In Matthew 10:18 He said, "You will be dragged before governors and kings for my sake, to bear witness before them and the Gentiles." If human government always fulfilled its divine responsibility of rewarding good and punishing evil, Jesus' prediction would've been unnecessary. But this is a fallen world with sinful rulers. Sometimes a government may do its job, and the righteous are defended. And often the scene Jesus describes in Matthew 10 becomes a painful reality.

Even though the apostle Paul wrote the premiere passage on human government in Romans 13, and even though he remained in subjection to the governmental authorities his entire life as a faithful Roman citizen, he still was executed. And he wasn't alone. The

Neronian persecution against Christians, launched in AD 67, was horrific. Believers were rounded up, tortured, and fed to wild beasts in the Coliseum or covered with pitch and lit as torches for parties. The persecution under Diocletian in AD 303 was worse.

> All the Christians were apprehended and imprisoned; and Galerius privately ordered the imperial palace to be set on fire, that the Christians might be charged as the incendiaries, and a plausible pretense given for carrying on the persecution with the greater severities. A general sacrifice was commenced, which occasioned various martyrdoms. No distinction was made of age or sex; the name of Christian was so obnoxious to the pagans that all indiscriminately fell sacrifices to their opinions. Many houses were set on fire, and whole Christian families perished in the flames; and others had stones fastened about their necks, and being tied together were driven into the sea.[8]

A march through church history reveals a long and sordid array of government-sponsored persecutions, its survey not showing rulers who understand and fulfill their God-given purpose. When persecution comes in America we shouldn't necessarily expect our government to protect us. The current cultural trends show protection isn't likely.

WHAT ABOUT CIVIL DISOBEDIENCE?

Both Romans 13 and 1 Peter 2 call us to submit ourselves to our governing authorities, for in doing so we show submission to God. No exceptions are listed. It is clear that the believer's general obligation is to obey the government. Is it ever permissible to disobey our governing authorities? Yes, but only when obeying man's law requires you to disobey God's law.

We have several biblical examples. The first occurred in Egypt when the Hebrew midwives were commanded by Pharaoh to murder the newborn Hebrew boys (Ex. 1:16). The midwives "feared God" (v. 17, 21), disobeyed Pharaoh, and God blessed them with families for their obedience (v. 21).

In Babylon, King Nebuchadnezzar commanded all the leaders of his empire to bow down and worship a ninety-foot-tall golden statue he erected in the plain of Dura (Dan. 3:1–6). Three Hebrew refugees—Shadrach, Meshach, and Abednego—refused to bow down, aware it violated God's law. They boldly proclaimed, "We will not serve your gods or worship the golden image that you have set up" (v. 18). God honored their courage by delivering them from the fiery furnace.

In Acts, Peter and John were arrested by the religious leaders and put on trial before the Sanhedrin (4:5–6). Stunned by their boldness but aware they were uneducated fishermen, the council commanded them "not to speak or teach at all in the name of Jesus" (v. 18). The two disciples responded, "We cannot but speak of what we have seen and heard" (v. 20).

IS IT EVER permissible to disobey our governing authorities? Only when obeying man's law requires you to disobey God's law.

In chapter 5, when they're brought before the Sanhedrin again, the high priest says, "We strictly charged you not to teach in this name." Peter answers and says, "We must obey God rather than men" (vv. 28–29).

Clearly the Bible allows for civil disobedience in limited situations. But it's limited. We're to obey our governing authorities even if we passionately disagree with the law. We can dislike high taxes, but we're to pay them. We can grumble about low speed limits, but we're to obey them. The only allowance for disobedience is if obeying their law requires us to disobey God's law.

Americans have rarely faced that decision. But what if the government required churches to perform same-sex marriages or lose their tax-exempt status? What if they required Bible colleges to hire transgendered faculty or lose their accreditation? That's not impossible.

If and when this occurs, we cannot expect the government to protect us. Although the government has the divine purpose of rewarding those who do good and punishing those who do evil, *we'll be exposed not protected.*

WHEN FAMILY TURNS ON YOU

It's hard for us to imagine our earthly family turning against us and becoming our persecutor. The family unit is valued as an environment of love, nurturing, and protection. When all others abandon us, we can usually count on our family to care and provide. This is God's design: parents who lovingly nurture and teach their children (Eph. 6:4) and children who honor and obey their parents (vv. 1–3).

Knowing that, verses such as Matthew 10:21 give us pause. In the context, Jesus is giving initial instructions to His disciples before sending them out to minister in His name. The picture of persecution He paints beginning in verse 6 is unpleasant, to say the least. The prediction about family must make us shudder! He says, "Brother will deliver brother over to death, and the father his child, and children will rise up against parents and have them put to death."

Christ identifies each family relationship: the relationship between siblings, parents and their children, and children and their parents. In each case Christ predicts hostility and betrayal. Family members won't lovingly protect one another; they'll turn on each other, concerned only with saving their own skin. Penner is correct when he says, "In societies where family loyalty and parental honor were paramount (like the Jewish society), these words must have sounded unbelievably harsh."[9]

Jesus' words are hard for us too. The last place we would expect hostility is in our own household. It forces us to realize that, for a disciple of Jesus Christ, mission takes precedence over family. Later Jesus explains, "For I have come to set a man against his father, and a daughter against her mother, and a daughter-in-law against her mother-in-law. And a person's enemies will be those of his own household. Whoever loves father or mother more than me is not worthy of me, and whoever loves son or daughter more than me is not worthy of me" (Matt. 10:35–37).

Jesus tells us persecution will strain family relations. Loyalties will be dumped, and personal survival will take precedence. As with the government, when persecution comes, we won't be able to expect our family, especially if they are unbelievers, to protect us. We will be exposed, not protected.

WHEN FRIENDS DESERT YOU

The isolation entering with persecution will be complete with the desertion of our friends. As with the government and our family, we won't necessarily be able to count on our friends to protect us. In Matthew 10:22, Jesus makes this comprehensive statement: "And you will be hated by all for my name's sake." It will get intensely lonely when your enemies start gathering. Comrades who previously stood with you will abandon you. Colleagues who supported you will desert you. When you face persecution and the emotional pain feels overwhelming, you'll turn to others for encouragement and counsel—and find no one there.

Paul experienced this in his second imprisonment. Unlike his first stint in prison, when he was free to receive visitors in his own rented quarters, his second arrest landed him in a dank, crowded Roman cell, facing certain execution.

His hopeless situation apparently led former associates to forsake him. In his second letter to Timothy, Paul wrote, "You are aware that all who are in Asia turned away from me, among whom are Phygelus and Hermogenes" (1:15).

The reference to those in Asia was purposely vague, but certainly included the church in Ephesus, where Paul had invested so much energy. The verb *turned away* (*apestraphesan*) can mean simple aloofness or total desertion. Paul probably experienced both. When you're in a cell, the practical effect is the same.

Hiebert makes this comment: "It would seem that Paul had written to Ephesus asking that some of his old acquaintances, men thoroughly familiar with his work and teaching, should come to Rome to testify on his behalf. But the apparent hopelessness of Paul's position and their fear of the possible consequences to themselves, had caused all of them to disregard the appeal."[10]

Paul wasn't totally abandoned, as he rejoices in the next verse that Onesiphorus had put aside the fear of Paul's chains and often visited him (v. 16). But for the most part, Paul was alone. Despite a ministry reaching to the ends of the Roman Empire, at the end of his life most of his friends did nothing to support him.

We should not be surprised to find the same thing happening to us.

EXPECT TO BE EXPOSED

When we face unjust persecution in the future, we'd like to believe a large crowd of people would protect, encourage, and defend us. We'd like the government to protect us from unfair punishment. We hope our family would support us in painful circumstances. We're sure our lifelong friends would stand boldly in our corner.

In some cases, that may happen. But we can't expect it. We can expect to be exposed, not protected. Others' desertion will put intense pressure on us to defect from the faith when persecution comes. We will so yearn to regain lost relationships, we will ponder abandoning Jesus. The readers of the book of Hebrews considered this when they faced persecution. It's easy to criticize them from a distance, but we soon may find ourselves in their shoes. All alone.

6

COMPASSION NOT ANGER

Bless those who persecute you;
bless and do not curse them.

ROMANS 12:14

Unless you're a masochist, suffering isn't enjoyable. It hurts! Rationally we know that in this sin-slogged, curse-ridden world, we cannot completely avoid pain. A twisting tornado doesn't differentiate between homes of believers and unbelievers. If you are in its unpredictable path, your house gets leveled. A drunk driver doesn't veer recklessly down the highway aiming for cars driven by the unsaved. If you have the misfortune of being on the road when he's inebriated, your new Chevy can end up in a head-on collision. It's not just non-Christians who hear the tragic news from their doctor that the medical tests show an inoperable form of cancer.

But if we're suffering unjustly, if we've experienced pain and persecution despite doing nothing wrong—or in fact, doing everything right—every bone in our body wants to scream in protest. We want to fight back. We want to lash out at our opponents and inflict an equal measure of pain on their heads. We want to return hostility with a similar-sized helping of anger. We can admit that.

This brings us to the fourth biblical, counterintuitive principle about persecution. *God calls us to respond to our persecutors with compassion, not anger.* He commands us to love them, not curse them.

But how, in our humanity, can we do this?

Christ left us a model to follow. He understands the pain of our dilemma. Although sinless, He suffered accusations, beatings, humiliation, and ultimately crucifixion between two common crooks.

> **IF WE'RE suffering unjustly, every bone in our body wants to scream in protest.**

Yet Peter wrote, "When he was reviled, he did not revile in return; when he suffered, he did not threaten" (1 Pet. 2:23).

Compassion, not anger. The ability of God's people to turn persecution into opportunities for the Gospel depends on embracing this principle. So does the mission Christ gave us. While it's counterintuitive, we cannot ignore it. Three times in the New Testament we find similar words of instruction—once each by Jesus, Paul, and Peter.

JESUS' COMMAND: LOVE YOUR ENEMIES

In the Sermon on the Mount, recorded in Matthew chapters 5–7, Jesus explains a new kingdom ethic to His followers. While He regularly repeats the formula, "You have heard it was said" (5:21, 31, 33, 38, 43), Jesus doesn't advocate an abolition of the Law for He states every jot and tittle will be fulfilled (vv. 17–18). Instead, He seeks to liberate us from a legalistic understanding of God's Word, so we don't follow the letter of the law yet also excuse ungodly behavior.

In this sermon, after addressing sensitive topics including adultery, divorce, and oaths, Jesus gives instructions on how God wants us to respond when others harm us. "You have heard that it was said, 'An eye for an eye and a tooth for a tooth.' But I say to you, Do not resist the one who is evil. But if anyone slaps you on the right cheek, turn to him the other also. And if anyone would sue you and take your tunic, let him have your cloak as well. And if anyone forces you to go one mile, go with him two miles" (vv. 38–41).

This is tactical advice followed by specific examples. If Jesus stopped there, we'd be tempted to limit our response to a donated cloak, a turned cheek, and an extra mile. But He wants to give us not just examples, but a theology and philosophy of living. He continues, "You have heard that it was said, 'You shall love your neighbor and hate your enemy'. But I say to you, Love your enemies and pray for those who persecute you, so that you may be sons of your Father who is in heaven" (v. 43).

The first part of Jesus' quotation is from Leviticus 19:18: "You shall love your neighbor." The second half, "and hate your enemies," isn't in the Old Testament but represented the logical way rabbis interpreted the verse. This teaching wasn't inconsistent with the Old Testament, as verses including Psalm 139:21–22 call for God's people to "hate those who hate God." But that interpretation oversimplified life.

As Jesus explains, God doesn't intend His people to demonstrate antagonism toward their enemies, but to love them. We understand what this requires because we love our family and friends. Love is the warmest of human emotions. It seeks the best for and sacrifices for others.

But the rub is that, by definition, an enemy is "one not loved." The word *enemy* (*exthros*) is an adjective meaning "hostile."[1] Those who persecute us qualify as enemies—they're hostile to us. But Jesus says that, as redeemed children and citizens of a spiritual kingdom, we're to love them. We're to intentionally seek their highest good.

Furthermore, Jesus says we're not just to love our enemies, but also to pray for them. We're not only to extend them warmth and acceptance, we're also to seek God's blessing in their lives by interceding for them with the Father. Stephen did this with his last breath (Acts 7:60).

PAUL'S COMMAND: BLESS YOUR ENEMIES

In Romans 12, Paul expresses a similar command. This chapter is filled with instruction for the Christian life, as Paul follows his rich theological exposition of chapters 1–11 with practical commands. The injunctions come in rapid-fire fashion, including a command concerning our enemies. "Bless those who persecute you; bless and do not curse them" (v. 14).

Paul envisions an awkward situation where a believer encounters a personal opponent, a persecutor, or a hostile enemy. Facing confrontation, in a fleeting moment, the believer must decide how to respond. Paul's basic command is seen clearly in the verb repeated twice in the verse. He says, "Bless them."

BY DEFINTION, an enemy is "one not loved."

When you bless someone, you invoke God's blessing on them. Similar to Christ's command to pray for our enemies, blessing them means we're asking God to touch our persecutor with His divine favor. While it's easy to read and understand those words, we shouldn't be deceived into thinking they're easy to obey.

Morris writes, "It sets a very high standard for Christians. Paul is not saying simply that they should refrain from retaliating against persecutors or that they should forgive them. He is saying that they should actively seek their good as they pray for God's blessing on them."[2] Schreiner agrees. "In this instance, it is not difficult to understand the meaning of the text, but the injunction to bless those who persecute us is one of the most revolutionary statements in the NT and can be carried out only by the power of the Holy Spirit."[3] We must remember this as we prepare to experience persecution. Blessing our enemies is hard, but Paul proved it could be done (e.g., 1 Cor. 4:12–13).

The second part of verse 14 repeats the command and adds a

clarifying element: "Bless and do not curse them." To curse someone is the opposite of blessing them. When we curse them, instead of asking for God's favor, we're asking for God's punishment. But Paul reminds us we cannot seek their demise. As the redeemed who have experienced God's profound mercy, we're to pursue God's blessings and mercy for our enemies. Just a few verses later, Paul explains why we can't seek revenge. "Beloved, never avenge yourselves, but leave it to the wrath of God, for it is written, 'Vengeance is mine, I will repay, says the Lord' " (v. 19).

God will deal with persecutors in due time. That's His business, and He'll handle all matters with perfect justice. Our business is to bless our enemies—as challenging as it may be. "If your enemy is hungry, feed him; if he is thirsty, give him something to drink" (v. 20).

PETER'S COMMAND: BLESS YOUR ENEMIES

Peter reinforces the teaching of Jesus and Paul with a similar command in 1 Peter. In this epistle Peter provides more instruction for persecuted believers than any other New Testament book. Written around AD 63, it reflects the rapidly changing environment Christians faced in the Roman Empire. While believers had enjoyed a measure of tolerance and acceptance in the broader community, with Nero's rise to the throne it all evaporated, replaced with slander, persecution, and fiery trials.

Peter's purpose, as Penner aptly puts it, "is to instruct the believers there to stand firm in their faith in the midst of a society that not only resented the message of Christianity, but, increasingly, even the very presence of Christians."[4] The pagan Romans resented Christians because the believers didn't conform to the rest of society. They didn't participate in the pagan cultural practices that were considered the norm, therefore they were viewed as odd, peculiar, narrow, and deserving of societal punishment.

In Greek and Roman culture, religious festivals and social gatherings were often characterized by heavy drinking and sexual depravity of virtually every sort. To refuse to participate was seen as being odd at the very least. Most would have likely considered it an expression of religious rejection and the Christians as being rather judgmental.[5]

Knowing his readers had a healthy supply of enemies at their doorstep, Peter reveals the attitude they must show their persecutors. "Finally, all of you, have unity of mind, sympathy, brotherly love, a tender heart, and a humble mind. Do not repay evil for evil or reviling for reviling, but on the contrary, bless, for to this you were called, that you may obtain a blessing" (3:8–9).

> **GOD WILL deal with persecutors in due time. That's His business.**

There's the word again: *bless*. Peter says, don't return insult for insult. Don't answer blows with blows. Don't respond to attacks with counterattacks. Instead, when others persecute you, bless them. Look to heaven and ask for God's gracious and abundant blessing to fall on them.

To support this, Peter quotes from Psalm 34. "Whoever desires to love life and see good days, let him keep his tongue from evil and his lips from speaking deceit; let him turn away from evil and do good; let him seek peace and pursue it. For the eyes of the Lord are on the righteous, and his ears are open to their prayer. But the face of the Lord is against those who do evil" (v. 10–12).

Note the emphasis on controlling the tongue. When we've been treated unjustly we can easily let our tongues loose like Mrs. Cratchit in *The Christmas Carol*, when her husband asks her to drink to Ebenezer Scrooge, the founder of their feast. She angrily responds, "The Founder of our Feast indeed! I wish I had him here. I would give him a piece of my mind to feast upon, and I'd hope he'd have a good appetite for it."[6] We identify with her.

Peter tells us, "Keep your tongue from evil," and "Keep your lips from speaking deceit." We need to turn from that temptation and instead "seek peace" and "do good"—intentionally, purposefully, and regularly asking God to bless those who persecute us.

> The persecuted are to be in service to those who cause them the suffering. Just as the Father gives light and rain to those who revile Him and refuse to love Him, so are His children to bring blessings to those who curse them, seeking the good for those who seek only to do them harm.[7]

The New Testament's teaching is clear, although it cuts against the grain of our emotions. Jesus, Paul, and Peter all echo the same challenging command: Respond to your persecutors with compassion, not anger. Bless them—don't curse them.

THE REASON FOR OUR RESPONSE

Knowing this, our obvious question is, "*Why* does God want us to show compassion to our enemies? What divine purpose does this serve?"

The answer is tied to our mission. God is "not wishing that any should perish, but that all should reach repentance" (2 Pet. 3:9). He commanded us as His children to be salt and light to the world. One of the most powerful—of many—ways we impact our enemies and influence them for the Gospel is through our response to persecution. A godly response provides us with a cherished opportunity to share the good news.

Peter teaches us this. After calling us to bless our enemies in verses 8 through 12, Peter continues to explain how our righteous behavior opens doors for the gospel.

Now who is there to harm you if you are zealous for what is good? But even if you should suffer for righteousness' sake, you will be blessed. Have no fear of them, nor be troubled, but in your hearts honor Christ the Lord as holy, always being prepared to make a defense to anyone who asks you for the reason for the hope that is in you; yet do it with gentleness and respect, having a good conscience, so that, when you are slandered, those who revile your good behavior in Christ may be put to shame. For it is better to suffer for doing good, if that should be God's will, than for doing evil. (vv. 13–17)

This passage, which provides vital understanding on a godly response to persecution, breaks down into two parts. In verses 13 and 14a, Peter reminds us of the reality of hostility. We should expect persecution. In 14b–17 he explains three ways God wants us to respond to hostility.

Peter begins by asking a rhetorical question: "Who is there to harm you if you are zealous for what is good?" (v. 13). The answer is left unstated, but is understood to be, "No one! No one should harm us if we prove zealous for what is good. For if we are zealous for what is good, that good should be recognized as good by everyone around us."

The government shouldn't harm us if we're zealous for good because, as we saw in Romans 13, God tasked the government to reward good and punish evil. If we do good, the government should applaud our efforts.

And society shouldn't harm us if we do good, because God placed within mankind a moral code ensuring God's creatures instinctively sense right and wrong. If you help the poor, that's right. If you rob the poor, that's wrong. Mankind has this code within them and, in an ideal world, if we do what is right and good, we shouldn't fear punishment.

However, as we're painfully aware, life in a fallen world isn't ideal.

Since we live in a world scarred by sin's curse, we *can* suffer for doing good. Peter admits this. "But even if you should suffer for righteousness sake, you will be blessed" (v. 14). In this verse he uses a rare verbal form (optative) that essentially says, "You shouldn't suffer for doing good in an ideal world. But in our fallen world, it could happen. And if you should suffer, you're blessed."

So Peter admits the chance of suffering is real. People zealous for good can and do face persecution, because good acts expose wrong acts. Righteous deeds reveal unrighteous deeds. People want to avoid that embarrassment; they don't want their evil deeds unmasked and to be exposed as a wrongdoer. So they attack those doing good. They reframe the issue so it appears those who are doing good are actually doing evil. A stance against abortion is cast as robbing women of their reproductive rights. Support for traditional marriage is viewed as discrimination against homosexuals. In a fallen world, hostility happens.

Fortunately, Peter provides three commands to help us face hostility in a godly manner.

Be Strong

Peter's first command is *be strong*. "Have no fear of them, nor be troubled, but in your hearts honor Christ the Lord as holy" (vv. 14–15a). Fear is normal when facing persecution because we don't know how it'll end. We wonder, will they hurt me? Will I lose my job? My friends? My freedom? Peter urges us to remember who's in charge. Our opponents aren't the judge and jury. Our Savior is Lord, and He rules over all—including our enemies. He'll take care of us. He loves us. We don't need to be afraid. Be strong.

Be Ready

Peter's second command: *be ready*. "Always being prepared to make a defense to anyone who asks you for a reason for the hope that is in you" (v. 15).

The word *defense* (*apologia*) is where we get our English words *apology* and *apologetics*. It's a word used in courts of law when a person would make a defense argument, as Paul did in Acts 22 and 25. Peter is using *apologia* in a broader sense and speaking of not just formal, courtroom defenses but also informal settings when people might question us.

This defense could happen anywhere—the streets, our home, the grocery store, or the local Starbucks. The question could come from anyone—friends, neighbors, relatives, or strangers. In every case and at all times, Peter commands us to be ready.

We should be ready because, when we respond to persecution in a godly manner and bless our enemies instead of cursing them, others will notice. Peter says they will ask us about it. Note: *they* will ask *us*—we won't have to initiate the conversation. They'll bring it up either because they are curious or furious. They'll ask because they know we're different. They'll inquire because they've been watching and can't figure us out. They'll wonder because, deep inside, they want to know why we act the way we do when we are unjustly treated.

When they ask, Peter says be ready. Be ready to give "a reason for the hope that is in you" (v. 15). In this context the *hope* is nearly synonymous with faith. When Peter says to give a reason for the hope in you he is saying, "be ready to explain your faith." Be prepared to explain the beliefs causing your zeal for good. Be ready to share the gospel. The question will be asked sincerely and could afford a golden opportunity to have a spiritual conversation with an unbeliever. We can't fumble the ball. For the sake of the kingdom we need to be ready.

The manner in which we respond matters. Peter says to give a defense, but do so "with gentleness and respect" (v. 15). *Gentleness* is often translated as meekness. The essence of meekness is strength under control. Likewise, we need to respect our enemies because, while perhaps manipulative and hostile, they're made in God's image. Despite their scars of sin, they are people Christ died for. Our attitude in responding is critical. We need to check our arrogance and anger at the door. God wants us to be His witnesses—not His prosecuting attorneys. Meekness and humility must undergird every word we speak.

Be Faithful

Peter's third command for responding to persecutors is to *be faithful*. "Having a good conscience, so that, when you are slandered, those who revile your good behavior in Christ may be put to shame. For it is better to suffer for doing good, if that should be God's will, than for doing evil" (vv. 16–17).

Our *conscience* is our inner witness that accuses us when we do wrong and confirms us when we do right. God wants us to keep a good conscience when we are accused by others. We need to live rightly, so when accusations come we know we're innocent. When the persecution begins, we know we don't deserve the punishment because we have a good conscience.

Peter says, with a good conscience we put our opponents to shame. This means all clearly see the charges were unfounded, and our enemies were shamefully wrong. Peter doesn't specify when this shame will occur. In our flesh we yearn for it to happen now, so our name is publicly vindicated.

> **WE CAN'T fumble the ball. For the sake of the kingdom we need to be ready.**

Sometimes this happens. If not, we can be assured it'll happen in eternity. Our persecutors will one day stand before God, the great judge who knows all things perfectly. When the books are opened, the truth will be evident and our opponents will be shamed for their treatment of us—if we keep a good conscience and are faithful.

ACTS: A STORY OF SUFFERING

A comprehensive understanding of persecution requires careful study of the book of Acts, because suffering runs through its entirety. Persecution starts in chapter 4—when the religious leaders threaten the apostles—and continues to the closing words of chapter 28 recounting Paul's imprisonment. The opposition included beatings, arrests, stonings, riots, and martyrdom.

In his research on the subject, Scott Cunningham sees five major theological themes on persecution emerging in Acts.[8]

1. **Persecution is part of God's plan.** Persecution is firmly located within divine providence. Jesus predicted His disciples would be persecuted, and those predictions were fulfilled. Persecution wasn't considered abnormal.

2. **Persecution is the rejection of God's agents.** In Acts, most of the opposition against the apostles comes from religious leaders. The ones who should've been considered the people of God end up hostile to the message of God. It's consistent with the rest of biblical history: God's people reject God's messengers.

3. **The persecuted stand in continuity with God's prophets.** The persecution experienced by Jesus and the apostles is a continuation of the suffering reaching back to the Old Testament prophets. In persecution, the disciples are in good company.

4. **Persecution is an integral consequence of following Jesus.** The apostles were persecuted because they claimed the name of Jesus. He's the conflict's focal point—not them. Persecution comes to the disciples not because they're guilty, but because of their association with Christ.

5. **Persecution is the occasion of divine triumph.** Opposition to the church doesn't extinguish it, but fuels growth.

Man may erect obstacles, but God always accomplishes His purposes. At the end of Acts Paul has taken the gospel to the ends of the Roman empire.

STEPHEN: "A TOUCH OF GOD'S GLORY"

The first martyr in church history was Stephen. His story, recorded in Acts 6 and 7, provides an example as we seek to respond to persecution with compassion instead of anger. Stephen stepped onto the stage of biblical history when he was the first named among seven men "of good repute, full of the Spirit and of wisdom" (6:5) to serve the tables of the Greek speakers in the early church. This enabled the apostles to devote themselves to preaching the Word of God. When the names are listed, Stephen is specifically described as a man "full of faith and of the Holy Spirit." The seven are named, commissioned, and released for ministry (v. 6).

While Stephen surely waited tables as he was called to do, he had a broader ministry of preaching and healing (v. 8). As he gave Spirit-filled witness of Jesus, opposition arose in Jews who had come from various locales. Some were freed slaves, some came from Alexandria of Egypt, some hailed from the Cyrenian region of North Africa, and others came from Asia. These Jews tried to dispute Stephen's teaching but, due to his Spirit-enablement, failed (v. 10).

Determined to silence Stephen, the Jews incited men to claim they'd heard Stephen "speak blasphemous words against Moses and God" (v. 11)—obviously a false charge. It created the intended negative energy, as it "stirred up the people and the elders and the scribes" (v. 12). Darrell Bock observes, "This is the first time in Acts that people rise up against Christians and not just challenge Christian leadership."[9]

The religious leaders seize (*synerpasan*) Stephen and drag him before the council for interrogation. The word *synerpasan* speaks of someone being pulled against his will and is used later in Acts (19:29) regarding the two men dragged with Paul into the Ephesian theater. It's unclear how formal the questioning was,[10] but it undoubtedly was an emotionally charged environment.

Violating the Mosaic law (Exod. 20:16; Deut. 19:16–18), Stephen's persecutors enlisted false witnesses. They claimed Stephen spoke against the Law and the temple. "This man never ceases to speak words against this holy place and the law, for we have heard him say that this Jesus of Nazareth will destroy this place and will change the customs that Moses delivered to us" (vv. 13–14).

While untrue as stated, the charges weren't baseless. F. F. Bruce says, "Jesus had indeed said something about destroying the temple, and Stephen had evidently repeated his words."[11] This stirred up the crowd more, for it was seen as an attack on the temple.

As Stephen faced his accusers, they were gazing at him and saw "his face was like the face of an angel" (v. 15). It's the only time in the New Testament this expression is used. Apparently Stephen's face was glowing. Bock writes, "It suggests Stephen has the appearance of one inspired by and in touch with God, reflecting a touch of God's glory."[12] It implies God considered Stephen innocent and pictures Stephen as calm, composed, and confident standing before his enemies.

The High Priest—probably Caiaphas—asks Stephen, "Are these things so?" The charges, if proved true, are serious. Speaking against the temple and the Law could lead others into apostasy. A response is needed from Stephen.[13]

Acts 7:2–53 records his response (his *apologia*), the longest speech in Acts. I won't dissect the sermon due to its length, but will note the two major themes.[14] Recounting the long history of the Jewish nation, Stephen first explains how Israel repeatedly rejected the leaders given by God. Joseph and Moses are included as prime examples. Second, Stephen explains the Jews didn't appreciate God's presence in both the tabernacle and the temple. Instead of leveraging the prescribed rituals into a deepened relationship, they fell away.

Stephen concludes by confronting the religious leaders. "You stiff-necked people, uncircumcised in heart and ears, you always resist the Holy Spirit. As your fathers did, so do you. Which of the prophets did your fathers not prosecute? And they killed those who announced beforehand the coming of the Righteous One, whom you have now betrayed and murdered, you who received the law as delivered by angels and did not keep it" (vv. 51–53).

It's not a gospel presentation, but it's a frontal statement about Israel's response to the righteous one God brought to them. Stephen ultimately brings them to the cross. He says "you rejected Him, like all the other prophets before Him, and you murdered Him." Bruce writes, "By rejecting the Messiah, they had filled up the measure of their fathers . . . in these last days, when God had spoken through no angel but through the Righteous One *par excellence*, Stephen's hearers had with even greater decisiveness rejected *him*"[15] (emphasis his).

The leaders' response to Stephen's charge was immediate and hostile. "Enraged" and "grinding their teeth," they rush him (vv. 54–57). Stephen remains calm despite the elevated antagonism, reflecting the control of the Holy Spirit.

After such a long scene, Stephen's death comes abruptly. The text simply says, "They cast him out of the city and stoned him" (v. 58). Before his voice was silenced under a barrage of stones, Stephen shows his compassion for his persecutors saying, in words reminiscent of Christ on the cross, "Lord, do not hold this sin against them" (v. 60).

THE MOST POWERFUL APOLOGETIC

In the face of persecution—execution—Stephen displayed compassion, not anger. Whether we can follow in his footsteps when angry opponents knock on our door is still unknown. We know our mission must remain central through suffering. Our response to opponents matters. The natural inclination to react with anger and defensiveness contradicts God's call to respond with love and compassion. If we can obey this call, we'll have opportunity to share the good news of Christ with those outside His grace. I echo the words of Penner, who writes,

> Why, then, are people who witness the love of God's people, the forgiveness that they demonstrate toward their enemies, and the courage and faith they exhibit in the face of trial and tribulation, drawn to faith in Christ? It is, of course, only because of the grace of God, drawing men and women to Himself, through His Holy Spirit, opening the eyes of the unbeliever to the truth of the gospel as His people demonstrate Christlike character. It is not because of any glory in the believers themselves. It is only because of what God has wrought in their lives as they live out the reality of Christ living in and through them. The most powerful apologetic is the faithful lives of God's people, demonstrating love, faith, and hope in the midst of a hostile world.[16]

7

REWARDED NOT FORGOTTEN

Blessed is the man who remains steadfast
under trial, for when he has stood the test
he will receive the crown of life.

JAMES 1:12

Society takes great pride in categorizing people as winners or losers. The winners have grasped the gold ring, climbed the corporate ladder, walked the red carpet, gained the multimillion-dollar contract, accomplished the high-stakes merger, bought the yacht, and made a name for themselves. They appear regularly on the covers of tabloids and above the fold in the *Wall Street Journal*. They're surrounded by expensive toys, beautiful people, press agents, and paparazzi. Millions follow their lives on Twitter, and many more yearn to have their fame and fortune.

Then there are the losers, seen as nondescript bumpkins who slug it out in a dead-end job, shop at Wal-Mart, stay married, serve on the local PTA, drive clunkers, and aren't recognized beyond their neighborhood. They spend their Saturday afternoon in the driveway installing brakes in their car—not golfing at an exclusive country club. Losers don't appear in photo ops with celebrities; they're in the serving line at the local soup kitchen. No one follows them on any form of social media—no one wants to.

No matter what financial success, corporate advancement, or public notoriety we've gained, when persecution comes to American believers our status will change. We'll be punished for our faith. It's possible we'll lose our jobs, our reputation, our family, our freedom, our health—even our lives. We'll feel like the dregs of society: misfits, outcasts, undesirable. We'll be viewed as losers.

Take heart. The fifth counterintuitive principle concerns our destiny. God promises that if we prove faithful in the midst of persecution, we'll be richly rewarded. The fifth principle is that *we'll be rewarded, not forgotten.*

THE REALITY OF ETERNAL REWARDS

The biblical teaching on rewards is severely neglected, even though the New Testament overflows with teaching on this subject. Sermons rarely touch it, so many believers are confused. They don't understand eternal rewards and wonder if they should seek them or not.

Rewards are different from our eternal salvation because entrance into heaven is a gift freely received by grace through faith in Christ. Once we believe, we're assured an inheritance "that is imperishable, undefiled, and unfading, kept in heaven for [us]" (1 Pet. 1:4).

> **WHEN PERSECUTION comes, we'll be treated like the dregs of society—losers.**

In contrast to the gift of salvation, rewards are earned. They're gained or lost based on our faithfulness in life. Jesus reminds us, "Behold, I am coming soon, bringing my recompense with me, to repay each one for what he has done" (Rev. 22:12).

Our rewards will be determined when we each stand before the judgment seat of Christ after we enter God's presence through death or the rapture. At the judgment—or *bema*—seat, each man's work will be fully and fairly evaluated by Christ Himself to reveal its value.

"Each one's work will become manifest, for the Day will disclose it, because it will be revealed by fire, and the fire will test what sort of work each one has done" (1 Cor. 3:13). If the judgment reveals faithfulness, we'll be rewarded, but if the judgment shows infidelity to Christ and self-indulgence, we'll forfeit our rewards. The judgment is individual; not everyone receives the same rewards. Lutzer comments,

> We should not conclude that every Christian will do well at the judgment seat of Christ. We can suffer serious loss; many of us might stand in shame before Christ as we see our lives pass before us. It is not true, as some teach, that ten minutes after our personal confrontation with Christ our meeting will have little significance because all of us will receive the same reward. What happens at the judgment seat can have permanent consequences.[1]

Scripture mentions a variety of rewards. Some bestow privilege such as authority in the Millennial Kingdom (Matt. 25:14–30). Others bring honor, such as the crowns mentioned repeatedly in the New Testament (e.g., 1 Pet. 5:1–4). Because they're given by our glorious Redeemer, all rewards are worthy of our lifelong pursuit.

THE PROMISE OF REWARD FOR SUFFERING

God promises He'll reward those who suffer persecution. In the Beatitudes portion of the Sermon on the Mount Jesus says, "Blessed are you when others revile you and persecute you and utter all kinds of evil against you falsely on my account. Rejoice and be glad, for your reward is great in heaven, for so they persecuted the prophets who were before you" (Matt. 5:11–12).

Beatitude people aren't problems to society. As described in previous verses, a beatitude person is poor in spirit, gentle, meek, gracious, and merciful. He's a peacemaker, not a troublemaker. Yet Jesus says these people will be persecuted like the prophets. He predicts three kinds of abuse.

JESUS PREDICTS VERBAL ABUSE

"They will revile you," Jesus warns. At its most literal, the verb *revile* means "to upbraid or insult someone." We can expect our opponents to take advantage of every opportunity to cast reproach on us and denigrate us in others' eyes.

Jesus spoke from experience. After His arrest in the garden of Gethsemane, His oppressors stripped Him of His clothes, wrapped a purple robe around His shoulders, pressed a crown of thorns onto His head, shoved a reed in His hand, and mocked Him, "Hail, King of the Jews!" (Matt. 27:28–29). That's verbal abuse; we should expect the same.

JESUS PREDICTS PHYSICAL ABUSE

He says in Matthew 5:11 that they will "persecute you." The attack moves from words to actions. It goes beyond insults to physical punishment. This was normal life for the apostles, and Paul could barely account for all his physical abuse (2 Cor. 11:23–25). Again, we can expect similar treatment.

JESUS PREDICTS FALSE ACCUSATIONS

They will "utter all kinds of evil against you falsely on my account" (Matt. 5:11). Paul was accused of being a rabble-rouser (Acts

16:20), treachery against Rome (17:7), and defiling the temple (21:28). Some Romans accused the early church of cannibalism because they spoke of eating Christ's body and drinking His blood in the Lord's Supper.

Verbal abuse. Physical abuse. False accusations. As followers of Christ, as beatitude people, we'll be persecuted.

But Jesus says, don't be mad or sad when abuse comes—be glad. "Rejoice and be glad, for your reward is great in heaven, for so they persecuted the prophets who were before you" (Matt. 5:12). When Jesus calls us to be glad, He doesn't mean we should crack out a weak smile or a nervous titter. He tells us to be *exceedingly* glad—the word is in the intensified form. It's the only time this word is used this way in the entire New Testament. It means we are to be super-abundantly, overflowing, exceedingly overjoyed persecution knocked on our door.

Jesus gives two reasons why such an attitude isn't upside down.

WHY BE GLAD?

Persecution Puts Us in Great Company

The Old Testament prophets were also persecuted: Jeremiah, Ezekiel, Isaiah, Daniel. God entrusted His revelation to them. The prophets were the great orators who stood before the world and proclaimed His message. They were the giants of the faith, highly esteemed by Jews at the time of Christ.

But they weren't revered when they were prophesying. They were persecuted and punished. The Israelites put Jeremiah in stocks in the public square and later tossed him into a cistern. Daniel landed in a lion's den. Isaiah was spurned and mocked by the kings of Israel. Instead of being widely received, their witness was soundly rejected.

When we suffer for our faith, we're in great company. We're locking arms with God's servants—His prophets—through history.

Persecution Brings Us Great Reward

"Be glad, for your reward is great in heaven" (Matt. 5:12). Christ promises that persecution for righteousness' sake brings reward. The reward is in heaven, so we cannot expect it on earth. And the reward is great; it won't be small or adequate—it will be abundant! This assures us that no matter how much pain and suffering persecution brings us in this life, it'll be dwarfed by the reward God gives when we come into His presence.

In Mark 10, Jesus emphasizes the greatness of the reward we'll gain if we suffer for His sake. The greater context of the passage is the demands of discipleship. A wealthy man asks Jesus, "Good Teacher, what must I do to inherit eternal life?" (v. 17).

The man is asking what works guarantee eternal life. Jesus answers his question by asking another question and then reciting six commandments from the Law. The man, apparently devout, claims he's kept the commandments from his childhood. So Jesus gazes at him—not with incredulity, but with love—and says, "You lack one thing: go, sell all that you have and give to the poor, and you will have treasure in heaven; and come, follow me" (v. 21).

The verse's language shows the commands are intertwined. Jesus says, "Sell and follow." The commands show the sacrifice necessary to follow Jesus. The man hears and grieves because he couldn't give up his many possessions.

As the dejected rich man walks away, Jesus seizes the moment to teach His disciples. He says, "How difficult it will be for those who have wealth to enter the kingdom of God!" (v. 23), which sparks amazement in the disciples. They hadn't come from the wealthy strata of society (except perhaps Matthew as a tax collector), but they were still stunned by Christ's words. Seeing their astonishment, Jesus continues, "Children, how difficult it is to enter the kingdom of God! It is easier for a camel to go through the eye of a needle than for a rich person to enter the kingdom of God" (vv. 24–25).

Christ's metaphor of a camel and needle is meant to be taken literally. Just as difficult as it would be for the largest animal in that society (a camel) to go through the smallest of openings (the eye of a sewing needle), so it's immensely difficult for a rich man to enter heaven. This doesn't discount grace or express prejudice toward wealthy people. It simply recognizes that affluent people, because of their many creaturely comforts, often struggle to recognize their need for a Savior. Christ's statement increases the disciples' astonishment, for it contradicted the prevailing teaching among the rabbis that material blessing indicated favor from God.

This sets the stage for Peter's great question. He's mulling over the requirement Jesus gave the rich man—that he walk away from all his riches and come follow Him. Peter knows he gave up his fishing business in Capernaum (Matt. 4:18–22), just as the other disciples forfeited their livelihoods. Mark's account doesn't record Peter's question. It only lists his declaration: "See, we have left everything and followed you" (Mark 10:28). Matthew's gospel includes Peter's question: "What then will we have?" (Matt. 19:27).

I love his question—not only for its honesty, but because it reflects what most believers ponder sometimes. "What's in it for me? What reward will I have for sacrificing to follow You? What'll I gain by giving up everything?" While we already ask those questions, they will become more pressing when persecution comes. Most American Christians, save those who obediently became cross-cultural missionaries, haven't given up much. Our faith has been an asset. But this will radically change as hostility ramps up. Thus, Peter's question is real and practical: What then will we have?

Jesus gives Peter a lengthy response. The second part reads, "Everyone who has left houses or brothers or sisters or father or mother or children or lands, for my name's sake, will receive a hundredfold and will inherit eternal life" (Matt. 19:29). Clearly Jesus is talking about rewards, for He follows with the parable of the laborers in the vineyard in Matthew 20:1–16. Mark ties the reward to persecution, for in his rendition he says, "Brothers and sisters and mothers and children and lands, *with persecutions . . .*" (Mark 10:30, emphasis mine).

If we're forced to surrender creaturely comforts or relationships in the future because of our identification with Christ, God won't forget the sacrifice. He'll remember, and it'll be evident when our life is carefully reviewed by Jesus at the judgment seat. Sacrifices made will endure as precious jewels when tested by fire. Based on the fire's revelation, Christ will reward us. The reward won't merely replace our losses. When Christ rewards us, it will be abundantly more than what we sacrificed. It'll greatly exceed what we surrendered to be His disciples.

> **MOST BELIEVERS sometimes wonder, "What's in it for me? What reward will I get for sacrificing everything to follow You?"**

THE CALL TO PERSEVERE

The promise of reward from God comes with a condition. He promises to significantly reward us, but the promise carries a requirement of perseverance through persecution. We'll be rewarded *if* we faithfully endure.

The writer of Hebrews presses this point in chapter 10. This epistle went to Jewish Christians experiencing sharp persecution from a variety of sources. They were dealing with ostracism, rejection, and humiliation. As Jews they'd once frequented the synagogue. As believers in Christ they'd left the Jewish religious system, which undoubtedly brought overt pressure from family and friends. Some believers were arrested and imprisoned; many had grown weary of the endless hostility and wanted to quit. Penner captures the historical setting well when he says, "In the face of such difficulties, these

Jewish-background believers had begun to struggle with the cost of discipleship and reconsider their decision to become followers of Jesus. They considered returning to their Jewish religious beliefs."[2]

The writer of Hebrews calls readers back to a full commitment to Jesus. The book's argument, which weaves in significant Old Testament imagery, builds to a powerful climax in its final chapters. Chapter 11 is one of the most famous chapters in the Bible, recounting saints from the past who lived by faith despite extreme challenges. Noah, Abraham, and Moses headline the list. Building on this legacy, the opening verses of chapter 12 charge readers to "run with endurance the race that is set before us" (v. 1).

Before this climax, in the final verses of chapter 10 the author explains why the readers had to persevere in hardship. If they didn't, they'd forfeit their reward. To encourage them to press on, he reminds them of the past. "But recall the former days when, after you were enlightened, you endured a hard struggle with sufferings, sometimes being publicly exposed to reproach and affliction, and sometimes being partners with those so treated. For you had compassion on those in prison, and you joyfully accepted the plundering of your property, since you knew that you yourselves had a better possession and an abiding one" (vv. 32–34).

We don't know how long these readers had been believers. Likely they had been Christians for a period of years, because the writer brings to their memory "the former days." Those previous years, as he describes them, had been difficult. They had "endured a hard struggle with sufferings."

This indicates that the readers had experienced public censure and physical affliction. The verbal reproach probably came mostly from their Jewish family and friends. The physical abuse probably originated from the Roman authorities as the empire developed greater contempt for Christianity. There were limits to the physical mistreatment they had experienced, for the writer reminds them they "have not yet resisted to the point of shedding your blood" (12:4). None of them had been martyred. It'd been painful, but not deadly.

Despite past hardship, the readers had done well. The author lists three admirable actions from their previous years.

1. Identification with Others

They willingly identified with others who were wrongfully treated (10:33b). The writer says they were *partners* (*koinonia*) with them, suggesting a deep fellowship versus a superficial relationship. The readers weren't ashamed of their persecuted brethren. They didn't distance themselves from the ones being punished as the disciples did at the garden of Gethsemane. Instead, they stayed in fellowship with their brethren and shared in their struggles.

2. Sympathizing with Others

The readers sympathized with believers who were arrested. Verse 34 says, "You had compassion on those in prison." We know some in the community had been arrested—perhaps much as Peter and John in Acts 4. The word *compassion* is the Greek word *sympatheo* from which we get our English word *sympathy*. It literally means "to have a fellow feeling with." Whatever pain and struggles arrested believers experienced, the readers wholeheartedly shared it. They habitually sympathized with them.

3. Acceptance of Loss

The third stellar practice from the Hebrew readers' past: they joyfully accepted their property being plundered (10:34). This loss may have come from judicial actions or from opportunistic looters. The end result was the same: their possessions were gone and they're forced to manage life's daily demands from a compromised position. The writer specifically notes they were joyful, not resentful.

How could they be joyful in the public seizure of their property?

The text says they knew they "had a better possession and an abiding one" (v. 34). This shows their eternal inheritance was real to them. Convinced of its reality, the readers happily parted with their temporal possessions. The earthly loss didn't depress them because they had a firm grip on their eternal rewards in Christ.

This means they epitomized the Sermon on the Mount's command when Jesus said, "Do not lay up for yourselves treasures on earth, where moth and rust destroy and where thieves break in and steal, but lay up for yourselves treasures in heaven, where neither moth nor rust destroys and where thieves do not break in and steal. For where your treasure is, there your heart will be also" (Matt. 6:19–21). Their heart was in heaven, and it didn't bother them to lose their earthly treasure.

All these Hebrews' past actions were admirable, and the writer applauds them. But despite their faithful past, if they didn't persevere, the text says they risk losing their rewards. "Therefore do not throw away your confidence, which has a great reward. For you have need of endurance, so that when you have done the will of God you may receive what is promised" (10:35–36).

The confidence the readers were about to toss away was a continuing trust in Christ. They were seriously considering a return to Judaism to escape the endless persecution. They'd come this far, but were ready to quit.

Knowing this, the writer passionately urges them to remain faithful and not toss aside their great reward. If they endure and do the will of God (persevere through persecution), he assures them that they'll receive the promised reward.

His point to them—and us—is clear: gaining eternal rewards demands perseverance. It'll get hard, but we cannot and must not quit.

STEADFAST UNDER TRIAL

James gives a similar message in James 1. As we already noted in earlier chapters, the trials referred to in this epistle were not your garden-variety struggles. The readers of the letter were facing significant opposition and persecution. Knowing this, the words of this verse are instructive to us: "Blessed is the man who remains steadfast under trial, for when he has stood the test he will receive the crown of life" (v. 12).

This verse reads as if it belongs in the Beatitudes—the flow of the verse is similar to Christ's words in Matthew 5:10: "Blessed are those who are persecuted for righteousness' sake, for theirs is the kingdom of heaven." The two differences, however, are significant.

James emphasizes the necessity of perseverance in our trials.

James says a man is blessed if he "remains steadfast" in his trials. Verb tenses always have meaning in the Greek language, and here James uses a present tense verb. This tells us the brave steadfastness must continue until the ordeal ends. It doesn't mean we'll never experience failure, but it requires us to right the ship, confess the error, and refuse to surrender. Then we'll have stood the test.

The word used here speaks of being approved after a period of testing. In the ancient world, when coinage was not as sophisticated, coins were sometimes tested to determine their genuineness. James says steadfastness in the midst of trials provides the same test for us.

James clearly sets forth the reward for such perseverance.

He says, "When he has stood the test, he will receive the crown of life." This crown cannot be synonymous with eternal life; for this would mean only faithful, steadfast Christians gain entrance to heaven. This would contradict the rest of the New Testament, which happily proclaims we are saved by grace through faith, not a result of our works, which would be grounds for boasting (Eph. 2:8–9).

Instead, the crown of life is one of the rewards we store up in heaven. The *crown* (*stephanos*) is the victor's crown, typically a wreath placed on the winner's head after an athletic contest. It represents honor and glory. If we faithfully endure through the coming persecution, we also can obtain this reward at the judgment seat of Christ. But we must be steadfast.

PAUL'S CONFIDENCE

As the days melted away and his execution neared, Paul had confidence of eternal reward. He knew his life would soon end, for he writes in 2 Timothy 4:6, "For I am already being poured out as a drink offering, and the time for my departure has come." The drink offering, an image also used in Philippians 2:17, was the final act of the sacrificial ceremony.[3] The "pouring out" began with the trial's inception. Marshall writes, "The present experience of imprisonment and the trial that has already taken place are part of the process that leads to the end. Hence Paul can feel that the time of his departure is not far distant. His life blood will be poured out as a sacrifice for the sake of the gospel."[4]

Conscious of his imminent demise, Paul reflects on his life with joy and satisfaction. "I have fought the good fight, I have finished the race, I have kept the faith" (2 Tim. 4:7). Those three short phrases confirm Paul's perseverance to the end. He fought the fight and didn't give up. He finished the race and didn't quit. He kept the faith until his last breath. His example should motivate every believer:

To come to the end of your life knowing you have accomplished the task that God has called you to do is what all God's servants should strive toward. To know that you have lived your life as a sacrifice to God, giving life to others in the process . . . What a contrast to the all-too-common sentiment expressed by many at the end of their lives: "If only I had had more time. If only I had done more for God. If only my life would have counted more. If only I could live my life again, I would do it differently."[5]

Awash in the knowledge of a well-lived life, Paul feels confident of his eternal reward. "Henceforth there is laid up for me the crown of righteousness, which the Lord, the righteous judge, will award to me on that Day, and not only to me but also to all who have loved his appearing" (v. 8).

Paul knew a crown awaited him—the crown of righteousness. This isn't the righteousness of Christ because all believers, at the moment of faith, are clothed with His righteousness. Without it we can't enter heaven.

This crown is an eternal reward Paul gained through love for Christ, demonstrated through perseverance in trials. He knows he'll receive it when he stands before Jesus at the judgment seat. But it's not an exclusive reward. Paul tells us that the same crown will be awarded to all who persevere.

REAL WINNERS

Society's icons enjoy their lofty perch where they determine the world's winners and losers. Self-proclaimed judges prop up the winners and rave about their extraordinary achievements. They trash losers and pity their lack of value. In a culture rapidly growing hostile to Christianity, we can predict how Jesus' followers will be classified. We'll be the losers and outcasts perceived useless to the greater culture—except as objects of hate deserving punishment and plundering. We'll feel forsaken because in an earthly, temporal sense, we will be.

At that moment, it'll be tempting to believe our emotions and lose perspective, for grinding though life as an exile makes one weary. At those low points we might find ourselves asking the same question as Peter in Matthew 19, "We have left everything and followed you. What then will we have?" The answer: *rewards.*

The Bible reveals to us this fifth counterintuitive principle: *we will be rewarded, not forgotten.* Our God will remember all we've done and everything we've sacrificed, and He'll abundantly reward us. Rewards gained at the judgment seat far exceed the level of our suffering, for our generous God gives out of His riches. Once gained, rewards can't be lost. No moths, no rust, and no thieves will ever tamper with our reward. That means, regardless of what the world believes, we are winners.

PART THREE

Reasons for Hope

8

GOD OUR HELP

And after you have suffered a little while,
the God of all grace, who has called you to
his eternal glory in Christ, will himself restore,
confirm, strengthen, and establish you.

———

1 PETER 5:10

It looks like a recipe for depression. Our beloved nation wracked by cultural change, once-protected freedoms evaporating, the persecution of believers looming. Anyone with sense would either stock up on Valium or claim a cave in Montana.

But as Christians we can choose optimism over pessimism. We don't live in a closed system where we're forced to solve problems with only available, natural resources. Our open system lets us access the sovereign Lord's abundant resources; therefore, no matter how bleak the situation, we always have hope.

Here in part three I want to explore this hope, because there's plenty to encourage us in the battle.

In chapter 9 you'll read an inspiring letter from a leader of the persecuted church in Pakistan. He writes to American believers to describe his church's extreme suffering and explain how persecution strengthened and purified their church. While we don't know if our suffering will ever match theirs, we can find encouragement both in believers faithfully enduring persecution and in their prayers for us facing a new reality in America.

After the letter from the persecuted church, we'll survey the history of American revivals. We already observed that the answer to our national dilemma is spiritual, not political. The accelerating cultural trends will only be arrested if a spiritual revival sweeps America. As hearts change, societies change. Nineveh proves it (Jonah 3:5–9). Revivalism is a hotly debated subject in the Christian academy. I don't wish to add fuel to the fire, but I hope to nurture our commitment to pray God again powerfully visits our land.

But the hope provided in part three begins with realizing the help God gives us—as His children—through persecution. Scripture shows how each member of the Trinity provides gracious help and enablement to believers when they face opposition. As bullets start flying, this is good news.

THE HELP OF THE FATHER

God the Father helps us in persecution through giving confidence He's in sovereign control of whatever happens to us. So while our enemies may think they're calling the shots, we know our God rules. Nothing happens to us outside of His will.

The experience of the three Hebrew young men in Daniel 3 proves this. We touched on the story briefly in chapter 5, but it deserves a closer look.

Shadrach, Meshach, and Abednego were among the Israelites deported to Babylon by King Nebuchadnezzar in 605 BC when he sacked Jerusalem. Along with Daniel, they received three years of special training to prepare them for the king's service. In Daniel 2, Daniel interprets Nebuchadnezzar's dream, which pictures him as the head of gold on an impressive statue (v. 38).

The king apparently liked this picture because he sets up a ninety-foot tall, golden idol on the plain of Dura (3:1).[1] This would be an impressive sight in the middle of an open plain. The text doesn't indicate what the image represented. While suggestions range from a representation of Nebuchadnezzar (unlikely) to an obelisk with writing on the sides detailing his exploits, most likely the image was a Babylonian god such as Nebo or Marduk. This seems reasonable because Nebuchadnezzar doesn't just demand his officials to view the image, but worship it (v. 2).

The list of officials the king called to the statue's unveiling represents an international gathering of top political leaders. They're brought to the plain of Dura, fifteen miles south of Babylon, and given instructions (vv. 4–6). When the Babylonian band strikes up the music, they were to bow and worship the golden image. As motivation for the reluctant, Nebuchadnezzar says, "Whoever does not fall down and worship shall immediately be cast into a burning fiery furnace" (v. 6).

The furnace's purpose and proximity to the plain of Dura isn't clear. Charles Baukal makes a reasonable suggestion that the furnace melted the metal used to fabricate the image, which would give it the capacity to heat at a much higher temperature.[2] The furnace may have been within eyesight of the officials. They hear his demand, see the furnace's smoke, and know the choice before them: bow or burn.

The herald signals the maestro, and the music begins. Everyone in this massive, dignified audience prostrates before the idol—except three Hebrew young men. With the thousands of people present, it may have not been immediately evident to the king that these three deliberately defied his command. In case he overlooked the insubordination, jealous Chaldeans bring it to his attention. "There are certain Jews whom you have appointed over the affairs of the province of Babylon: Shadrach, Meshach, and Abednego. These men, O king, pay no attention to you; they do not serve your gods or worship the golden image that you have set up" (v. 12).

The sneer is evident in their voices. These Jews were part of a defeated nation and had no right to enjoy prominence in the Babylonian empire. This gave opportunity to put them back in their rightful place. Of the three charges leveled against Shadrach, Meshach, and Abednego, only the first was false. They did pay attention and listen to the king, even if they wouldn't serve his gods or worship the image.

The king responds as the Chaldean accusers hoped he would: with royal rage. He collects the three Hebrews, parades them before his throne, and asks, "Is this true? Will you not bow down before the image?"

He's in disbelief, as he gave them jurisdiction over the Babylonian province. Unsure of their intentions, the king gives the three a chance to save their lives. He'll cue the music again and, in his presence, they must prove their obedience. If they won't, Nebuchadnezzar declares their sentence: "If you do not worship, you shall immediately be cast into a burning fiery furnace. And who is the god who will deliver you out of my hands?" (v. 15).

Hit the pause button for a moment. You have three young men, imports to the culture, standing before the most powerful man on the face of the earth. Is it intimidating? Absolutely. We have nothing to compare this with in the United States. We live in a democracy, not a land controlled by evil despots. So as we anticipate future persecution, we know we face only what God's people experienced in the past.

The men's faith is unflinching. Despite Nebuchadnezzar's ultimatum, Shadrach, Meshach, and Abednego refuse to compromise. Their answer to the king is a primer for anyone facing persecution: "O Nebuchadnezzar, we have no need to answer you in this matter. If this be so, our God whom we serve is able to deliver us from the burning fiery furnace, and he will deliver us out of your hand, O king. But if not, be it known to you, O king, we will not serve your gods or worship the golden image that you have set up" (vv. 16–17).

These three men show a powerful grasp of God's omnipotence and sovereignty. They understand God's power, because they clearly tell the king, "Our God is able to deliver us." That's not a question in their minds. They know it's true—God has the power to deliver because He's omnipotent.

But they also understand God's sovereignty. While they know God is able to deliver them, they also know He may not. He's sovereign. He isn't obligated to rescue them. He never promised to save any believer who faces death for obedience to His Word.

Hearing their response, his face distorted with rage at their insolence, and the king heats the furnace to its maximum temperature.[3] Shadrach, Meshach, and Abednego are dropped into the kiln from the top, bound like logs in their own clothes.

As we know from our acquaintance with the story, God chose to deliver the Hebrews (vv. 19–27). God doesn't save them *from* the fire, but He protects *in the midst of* the fire. A fourth person, likely the pre-incarnate Christ, joins them in the furnace. The ropes binding the three are burned away, but the fire doesn't harm them. The asphyxiation, which would come immediately in a furnace consuming all the oxygen, is prevented. When they're retrieved, there's no smell of smoke on their clothes, nor has a single hair (intensely combustible) been singed.

God can deliver us from anything we face in the future. He's omnipotent. But we also need to be aware—as these three men were— that even though God *can* deliver us, He doesn't always *choose* to deliver us. Hebrews 11 confirms this. The chapter lists champions of the faith who trusted God in severe challenges. Some experienced deliverance and victory. The writer speaks of those who, through faith, "stopped the mouths of lions, quenched the power of fire, escaped the edge of the sword, were made strong out of weakness, became mighty in war, put foreign armies to flight"(vv. 33–34).

But there were others—likewise faithful—who were "tortured, refusing to accept release . . . Others suffered mocking and flogging, and even chains and imprisonment. They were stoned, they were sawn in two, they were killed with the sword. They went about in skins of sheep and goats, destitute, afflicted, mistreated—of whom the world was not worthy—wandering about in deserts and mountains, and in dens and caves of the earth" (vv. 35–38).

Sometimes the faithful escape; sometimes they're killed. How can we know if God will deliver us? We can't. We know He's omnipotent and we recognize He's sovereign, but we can't know how He'll act in our situation.

That said, God promises to give us wisdom at that moment if we ask Him for it. "If any of you lacks wisdom, let him ask God, who gives generously to all without reproach, and it will be given him" (James 1:5). While we've often applied this to any time we're seeking wisdom, the context shows its intended application is in trials. When we're at a trial's boiling point, we typically lack divine perspective. James admits this, because when he says, "If any of you lacks wisdom," it could be translated, "Since you lack wisdom," or "If any of you lacks wisdom (as you do)."

> **EVEN THOUGH God *can* deliver us, He doesn't always *choose* to deliver us.**

Wisdom differs from knowledge. Knowledge grasps the facts. We can know we're facing a hostile situation, but that doesn't mean we have the wisdom to rightly respond. Peter Davids says, "Wisdom . . . is the possession of the believer given by the Spirit that enables him to see history from a divine perspective."[4] When we have wisdom, we gain more of God's viewpoint on our suffering.

Fortunately, God offers wisdom to us freely. James says, "God gives (wisdom) generously to all without reproach." So we need to ask Him for it. Not once or twice, but every time we face angry enemies. God is the storehouse of wisdom and, since we lack it, we need to regularly request more from Him. He gives to us "without reproach," so we need not fear He'll be critical if we continually ask Him for more. God won't be demeaning because it's His nature to give and give generously. He encourages us to ask and ask and ask again. When we do, His response is, "I'm so glad you asked! Here it comes!"

The Father is an incredible help when we face persecution. He's omnipotent and sovereign; He can do anything He chooses. He loves us and offers wisdom in our trials if we ask. Our job is to trust Him and know He has sovereign control over all things.

THE HELP OF THE SON

The Son can also help us in persecution. As the One who became incarnate and dwelt among us, and who suffered and died for us, He provides a model to follow in suffering.

Appropriately, Peter uses Christ as an example for his readers, who were constantly in the crosshairs of their opponents. In 1 Peter 2, Peter couches this teaching in the context of household relationships which can produce suffering—specifically masters and slaves.

The principles are also intended for us, because Peter later reminds us suffering is expected for all who follow Jesus.[5] While some suffering may be due to our sinful behavior (v. 20; also 4:15), this passage's suffering is unjustified: "For this is a gracious thing, when, mindful of God, one endures sorrows while suffering unjustly. . . . If when you do good and suffer for it you endure, this is a gracious thing in the sight of God" (vv. 19, 20).

When following Jesus requires unjust pain and suffering, He's given us an example to follow. In verse 21, Peter gives us these powerful words: "For to this you have been called, because Christ also suffered for you, leaving you an example, so that you might follow in his steps." Three important principles emerge from this verse.

Suffering is our calling in Christ

While we may not enjoy it, suffering is our calling in Christ. When Peter says, "to this you have been called," the *this* links back to the unjust treatment in verse 19. Our calling appeared the moment we came to faith. When we trusted in Christ as Savior we also gained this calling from God. We cannot deny it; we must not avoid it.

Suffering has an example in Christ

Christ left us a pattern to follow when we suffer. Peter says, "Christ also suffered for you, leaving you an example" (v. 21). The word *example* (*hypogrammon*) is a rare word, plucked from the secular world by Peter and used only here in the New Testament. A compound word, consisting of the root *grammon*, which means *writing*, and the prefix *hupo*, which means *under*, the term literally means *underwriting*.[6]

Hypogrammon was used in education to describe how children learned to write the alphabet. They would trace over the pattern of the letters as they learned each stroke and shape. Here it implies a tight resemblance. Karen Jobes writes, "It suggests the closest of copies. English words such as 'example,' 'model,' or 'pattern' are too weak, for Jesus' suffering is not simply *an* example or pattern or model, as if one of many; he is *the* paradigm by which Christians write the large letters of his gospel in their lives."[7]

Suffering means following in the steps of Christ

We're to carefully, purposefully follow in the footsteps He's provided. Peter says Jesus left us an example "so that you might follow in his steps" (v. 21). The imagery here moves from the classroom to a snow-covered path. Jesus has gone before us as the suffering servant, leaving us footprints in the snow. His path is a good and righteous one, so fidelity insists that we follow His tracks. Since we're fallible humans, we cannot expect to place our feet exactly in His footprints, but we need to be heading in the same direction.[8]

How did Jesus respond His unjust treatment? "He committed no sin, neither was deceit found in his mouth. When he was reviled, he did not revile in return; when he suffered, he did not threaten, but continued entrusting himself to him who judges justly" (vv. 22–23).

Peter makes two main points about Jesus' response to suffering. First, *Jesus didn't retaliate.* He didn't return insults, threats, or attacks. He didn't sin physically or verbally. Second, Peter says *Jesus kept entrusting judgment to His Father.* God will set all records straight. His judgment will be perfect and impartial. We can trust God to exact whatever punishment may be due our opponents—if not in this life, then in the life to come.

Since Jesus left us the example to follow, when we suffer our eyes must be on the path He made for us. This is what Hebrews 12:1–2 says: "Therefore, since we are surrounded by so great a cloud of witnesses, let us also lay aside every weight, and sin which clings so closely, and let us run with endurance the race that is set before us, looking to Jesus, the founder and perfecter of our faith, who for the joy that was set before him endured the cross, despising the shame, and is seated at the right hand of the throne of God."

The writer of Hebrews, like James and Peter, desires his readers —and us—to run the race of the Christian life with endurance, despite continued persecution. How? He lists three strategic decisions we must make. The third decision is most important for our current topic, but let me briefly mention the first two.

Remember the Heroes

First, he tells us that if we want to run the race well we must remember the heroes. Remember the "great cloud of witnesses" who have gone before us, living by faith in spite of great difficulties. Some of the best examples are in Hebrews 11. I have no argument with Noah, Abraham, and Moses, and I look forward to meeting them in eternity.

But since the writing of Hebrews we've had two thousand years of church history. During those many centuries we've gained additional heroes whose faithful endurance is worth remembering when our energy starts to flag. People such as Jim Elliot, the martyred missionary, and Joni Eareckson Tada immediately come to mind. Your list can differ from mine. The point is, when we consider quitting we remember the heroes and keep running.

Drop the Weights

The second strategic decision we're to make if we want to run the race well is to drop the weights. "Lay aside every weight, and sin which clings so closely" (12:1). Weight inhibits you when you're running a race. Runners don't strap on extra armor before stepping to the starting line; they eliminate additional weight which could slow them down. Every ounce makes a difference.

Therefore, the writer says *drop the weights*. Lay it all aside—every encumbrance, sin, and habit that'll work against us in the demanding race before us. Weight can cling to us, so we need to kick it to the curb.

Keep Looking at Christ

The last decision we must make to run with endurance is to keep looking at Christ. The writer calls us to focus on Jesus. "Run with endurance . . . looking to Jesus, the founder and perfecter of our faith" (v. 2a). The *looking* he calls for isn't like the quick glance you take at your car's side mirrors to check if another vehicle is coming. This is a fixed and focused attention.[9] If we want to be steadfast through persecution, we must constantly look to Jesus.

Why? He's our model and example after He "endured the cross" (v. 2b). He did what we must do: endure temporal, physical pain for eternal glory. He willingly gave Himself up to endure the most degrading and humiliating form of execution man ever created in order to gain the prize (the joy) set before Him. And He left the trail—footprints to guide us. We don't have to face persecution wondering how God wants us to respond. Jesus helps us if we look to Him.

THE HELP OF THE SPIRIT

Like the Father and Son, the Spirit provides enormous help to believers when we're facing persecution. We can be comforted by the Father's sovereign control, guided by the Son's example, and also empowered by the work of the Holy Spirit. The Spirit can help us in our weakness if we rely on Him.

Paul provides helpful insight into the Spirit's work in Romans 8:26. This passage isn't typically applied to persecution, but a glance at the broader context shows this is exactly Paul's intent. A few verses earlier he repeatedly mentions suffering. In verse 17 he says we're fellow heirs with Christ "provided we suffer with him." Then he says, "For I consider that the sufferings of this present time are not worth comparing with the glory that is to be revealed to us" (v. 18). In verses 19–25 he explains that even creation is suffering and waiting for the day of its redemption.

Clearly, suffering is in view when Paul talks about the Holy Spirit. "Likewise the Spirit helps us in our weakness. For we do not know what to pray for as we ought, but the Spirit himself intercedes for us with groanings too deep for words" (v. 26).

Paul says "the Spirit helps us" in our weakness. The English translation to the word *help* is rather bland, as the Greek word—used rarely in the New Testament—means literally, "to lend a helping hand" or "to come to the aid of someone."[10] It suggests the Spirit comes beside us to help when the pain is overwhelming us, when we don't know what to pray.

While in seminary, I served as a pastoral intern in a Texas church. Late one night I received a tragic call. A college friend from church had lost his only sister in a head-on car accident. He received the news at a football game, and I raced to his house to be there and support him when he arrived.

When he pulled in, it was obvious the three-hour drive had tested his endurance. His eyes were red and swollen, his gaze a glassy stare, his walk a slow shuffle. I met him in front of the house, put an arm around him, and we stood silently in the driveway for a while. Finally he looked up and murmured, "Paul, I just don't know what to say."

When persecution comes, we may feel the same way with God in prayer. We'll be hurting so much we won't know what to say. The Holy Spirit helps by interceding for us when we—in our pain and weakness—don't know what to pray. Paul says "the Spirit himself" (repetition providing emphasis) "intercedes for us with groanings too deep for words." When we can't find words, the Holy Spirit puts His arm around us and communicates with the Father in ways we cannot fathom.

How do we know the Spirit's groanings communicate our needs to God? Paul explains, "And he who searches hearts knows what is the mind of the Spirit, because the Spirit intercedes for the saints according to the will of God" (v. 27). God knows the Spirit's mind as He intercedes, because God is omniscient. He doesn't need words from us; He understands a sigh, groan, or whisper. God's omniscience isn't dependent on our communication skills.

But the Spirit doesn't only communicate for us when we don't know what to pray; He also gives us the right words when we stand before our persecutors and want to testify about Christ. In chapter 3 we looked at John 15:18–25 where Jesus explained the world hates us because we're different, identify with Christ, and expose their sin. After that discouraging report Jesus concludes by sharing encouragement. He explains the Spirit will help by giving us words to witness to our hostile opponents. "But when the Helper comes, whom I will send to you from the Father, the Spirit of truth, who proceeds from the Father, he will bear witness about me. And you also will bear witness, because you have been with me from the beginning" (John 15:26–27).

We live in a world that hates us, but we have a Helper. The word for *helper* means "comforter" or "intercessor." The Spirit has been sent to us specifically to bear witness about Christ. He wasn't sent to promote Himself; His mission is to herald Christ through the lives and lips of believers. When we face persecution and don't know what to say (or believe we have the courage to say it), if we rely on the Spirit within us He'll give us the words. If we depend on Him, He'll open our mouths, give us boldness, and use us to give testimony to Christ.

> **WHEN WE can't find words, the Holy Spirit puts His arm around us and communicates with the Father in ways we cannot fathom.**

Jesus made the same promise in an apocalyptic context in Luke 21:12–15. "They will lay their hands on you and persecute you, delivering you up to the synagogues and prisons, and you will be brought before kings and governors for my name's sake. This will be your opportunity to bear witness. Settle it therefore in your minds not to meditate beforehand how to answer, for I will give you a mouth and wisdom, which none of your adversaries will be able to withstand or contradict."

Jesus says the time before our persecutors will be a chance to witness of Him. While we may wonder whether we'll have the courage to speak, He says not to worry and promises us a voice and wisdom which will confound our opponents. How will He do this? Through the Holy Spirit.

The apostles experienced this Spirit-enablement in Acts 5. They'd been arrested and imprisoned by the Sanhedrin for preaching about Christ in the temple. They were strictly charged not to preach Christ anymore. With the tension in the room rising, Peter boldly rejects their command saying, "We must obey God rather than men" (v. 29).

How did he make such a bold statement in front of his adversaries? By the power of the Spirit. Three verses later he tells them, "And we are witnesses to these things, and so is the Holy Spirit, whom God has given to those who obey him" (v. 32).

Notice the theology. The disciples are witnesses of Christ—but so is the Holy Spirit. As a result, the church was born in the middle of a world that hated it.

"SUFFICIENT IS THINE ARM ALONE"

If America's cultural trends continue, the road before us won't be easy. We'll likely be rejected, marginalized, and persecuted simply because we're identified with Christ. With restrictions rising and freedoms disappearing, we could one day be accused of hate speech for being true to God's Word.

Our God sees our plight. In ways that will confound our enemies, He *can* and *will* help us. The Father will help us as we trust in His sovereign control and ask for wisdom. The Son will help us as we look to Him for a righteous model to follow. The Spirit will help us by giving us power and a bold witness when we rely on Him. We need nothing more.

Isaac Watts captured this encouraging truth in the classic hymn, "O God Our Help in Ages Past." The first two verses of the hymn read:

O God, our help in ages past,
Our hope for years to come,
Our shelter from the stormy blast,
And our eternal home.

Under the shadow of Thy throne
Thy saints have dwelt secure;
Sufficient is Thine arm alone,
And our defense is sure.

The stormy blast is coming. Be prepared. And remember—God will help us.

9

AN ENCOURAGING WORD FROM THE PERSECUTED CHURCH

Resist him, firm in your faith, knowing that the
same kinds of suffering are being experienced by
your brotherhood throughout the world.

1 PETER 5:9

A s American believers encounter an increasingly hostile culture,
it's helpful and encouraging to hear the testimony of Christians
from around the world who've faced and endured profound persecution. In this chapter, a leader in the Pakistani church tells his story to
not only acquaint us with the level of their suffering, but also explain
the gracious work God accomplishes through it. For security reasons,
he remains anonymous.

LIVING WITH PERSECUTION

Believers in my country of Pakistan have faced various forms
of persecution. One is the sociopolitical discrimination seen in the
historical class system on the Indian subcontinent. For instance, as
per the constitution of Pakistan, any non-Muslim is barred from

becoming the president or prime minister—thus reducing their status to second-class citizens.

Another form of persecution is the unjust laws which manifest in extreme religious intolerance. By 2013, over twelve hundred people were charged under the blasphemy laws. The majority of the charges were brought to settle personal scores, and often the cases were settled outside the court.

Persecution affects socioeconomic and socioreligious aspects of life for Christians in Pakistan. The majority of Christians fall in the lowest economic ladder; most conversions to Christianity in the early twentieth century were from the low-caste Hindus. These converts are not allowed to eat or drink with Muslims. When the government advertises new jobs for cleaners, they highlight these jobs are only for Christians. This blatantly discriminates against the poor Christians, and it keeps them in poverty and socially low-caste situations. To add insult to injury, these jobs are only given to people who can bribe the officials.

Many Christians working as brick makers are trapped in modern slavery. Being illiterate, they are unable to notice when their debts are deceitfully recorded. Often the church has paid off their debts and rescued them through legal aid, but this is an ongoing challenge and overwhelming task.

There have been countless incidents where young Christian girls working as domestic housekeepers are raped by Muslim employers. There is a common feeling among Muslims that these girls will never speak or stand up for their rights. Sometimes the girls are forced to marry their employers; by temporary marriages, Muslims avoid any legal prosecution.

One of the most brutal forms of persecution comes under the guise of blasphemy laws. *Section 295-B* states, "Whoever willfully defiles, damages or desecrates a copy of the Holy Qur'an or an extract there from or uses it in any derogatory manner or for any unlawful purpose shall be punishable with imprisonment for life." *Section 295-C* states, "Whoever by words, either spoken or written or by visible representation, or by any imputation, innuendo, or insinuation, directly or indirectly, defiles the sacred name of the Holy Prophet Mohammed (peace be upon him) shall be punished with death."

According to this law, anyone who speaks anything against the Prophet Muhammad is sentenced to death. Recent examples: One of my church members—Mr. AA—was arrested upon the complaint of a fundamentalist Muslim organization. He was taken to the local police station and tortured. Mrs. AG from my church was also arrested and tortured in the police station.

The effects of extremism on Pakistan have been many. After 9/11, several churches and Christian institutions were attacked. The first assault was on a church in Bahawalpur and left eighteen people dead. Attacks followed on Taxilla Hospital, Murree Christian School, the Protestant International Church Islamabad, and the Bible Society's office in Karachi. In addition, churches were burnt in Sukkur, Sangla Hill, and Peshawar. A Muslim mob attacked the Christian communities in Shanti Nagar, Korian, Gojra, Lahore Joseph Colony, and Mehrabadi Islamabad, and burned down their houses.

A Christian student was expelled from school because she misspelled an Urdu word that, instead of praising, insulted Muhammad, leading to accusations of blasphemy, which carries the death penalty. After the teacher beat her, the principal was notified and Muslims staged demonstrations demanding registration of a criminal case against the eighth-grader and her eviction from the area.[1]

As riots and violence were about to erupt, the military intervened: "They bundled the family in an ambulance and took them away."[2]

"A Christian high school teacher has suffered false accusations of blasphemy by a student and some Muslim professors, because of dislike, revenge and hatred towards Christians. He was forced to leave his job and hide, he appealed to the Court, but the laconic sentence of the judge of first instance invited him to leave the country."[3]

A thirty-year-old Christian man—accused of blasphemy and imprisoned—died in his cell from a treatable disease "after officials denied him proper medical care."[4] While in prison, he and others "accused of blasphemy, were kept in solitary confinement without access to a toilet, water or electricity."[5]

A Christian mother of five was raped by two Muslim men who "tend to assume they will not be prosecuted if their victims are Christians"; she and her family are being threatened with violence unless they drop the charges.[6]

A Christian nurse was raped by a Muslim colleague, who filmed the act in an attempt to blackmail her into renouncing Christianity and marrying him: "[he] raped me while his friend filmed the entire incident. They ruined my life completely."[7] Barnabas Fund, an advocacy group, estimates that every year seven hundred Christian girls are abducted and forced to convert to Islam and marry their abductors.[8]

Unfortunately, many Muslims consider Christianity a Western religion. Whenever something happens against Muslims in the world, Christians pay a heavy price and become a target of the Muslims' anger. Whether it was the Danish cartoons incident or the wars in Afghanistan and Iraq, the Christians in Pakistan bear the brunt of Muslim fundamentalist anger.[9]

My first experience of discrimination came in 1965 during fifth-grade summer school. Since my birth in 1956 I'd lived near Lahore, where mid-June temperatures can reach 120 degrees Fahrenheit. One hot summer day I was very thirsty and approached the water jar shared by Muslim students. When I attempted to drink, the students got angry and severely beat me. I was confused and sad, and I asked my father why I had to go through this pain. He encouraged me, and he told me to be patient and trust the Lord. This incident led me to leave the Muslim school and move to a Christian missionary school in Sialkot.

In 1965, war broke out between India and Pakistan. My village was bombarded by artillery shells from the Indian guns. Many houses nearby were destroyed, but by God's grace none fell on our house. This aroused the suspicion that we were Indian spies.

After multiple threats, my father was beaten in front of us. I was terrified, and this incident left a deep scar on my heart. Out of all the events during my childhood, this one remains vivid in my memories and still pains me.

STORIES FROM THE PERSECUTED CHURCH

After receiving my theological education from the Republic of Korea (South), God fulfilled the vision He had planted in me through the establishment of Grace Ministries in the Islamic Republic of Pakistan.

In spite of persecution and challenges, the Pakistani church kept growing. I started my ministry from the slum areas of Punjab in 1987. Both direct and indirect persecution have brought many positive outcomes for the church. First, it has strengthened the faith of believers and resulted in growth. Second, the persecution has inadvertently advertised the gospel throughout our country, which led many nonbelievers to question their own teachings and find their personal Savior.

Through persecution the believers were reminded and encouraged by the psalms of David. Psalm 23:4 says, "Even though I walk through the valley of the shadow of death, I will fear no evil, for you are with me; your rod and your staff, they comfort me."[10] Whether it was the attack on our Christian community, blasphemy cases against believers, or open discrimination in the public sphere, each incident brought us to our knees. The deeper the pain inflicted upon us, the stronger our reliance on God became.

I was the first church leader to arrive on the scene and witness the aftermath of the Gojra, Sangla Hill, Lahore Badami Bagh, and Peshawar All Saints Church incidents. Most recently I visited the victims injured in the Peshawar All Saints Church twin blasts to lift the spirits of families and pray with them in the hospital. It helped strengthen and restore their faith.

Despite some serious life threats, the prayers of my congregation encouraged me to be there for my suffering brothers and sisters. The local police and administration told me to stay away, as the risk of sectarian terrorism and mob violence was too high. However, the horrific sufferings of our fellow believers gave me strength to overcome any fear.

The gruesome persecution united our community, and there was an outpouring of love and support for their fellow brethren in pain. Our church members had raised financial support to distribute wheelchairs, hospital support beds, food supplies, and first-aid kits, as well as finance the relocation of the injured to proper medical facilities.

THE DEEPER the pain inflicted on us, the stronger our reliance on God became.

God paved the way for us to turn persecution into an opportunity to share the gospel. The youth and other church volunteers distributed one Bible per household with food supplies. With each first-aid kit we included Christian literature in local languages.

All of this suffering seems trivial in hindsight. Not only did our ministry grow tenfold, but there was tremendous growth in the Pakistani church. For example, I started my ministry from humble beginnings. We had no church building, and I was ministering among people in slum areas while possessing very limited resources.

Through these years of persecution we have grown stronger in faith, and now twenty-two congregations have been rooted and eighteen new churches have been built on the inspiration of Nehemiah, Ezra, and Paul. These churches have a combined membership of more than ten thousand people, and our ministry supports more than one hundred employees. Moreover, by the grace of God, we are also operating six small schools, two medical clinics, and have several social projects. All glory goes to the Father, the Son, and the Holy Spirit.

Through persecution, many Muslims are coming to Christ and finding peace in Jesus. Thirty-two Muslims have converted and received baptism. In the northeastern part of Pakistan, where the main language is Pashto, sixteen Muslims have come to Christ in the last three years. Some of the new converts are former Taliban; one was a Taliban imam (Muslim cleric).

Former Muslims go through intense persecution in every aspect of their life. Islamic law forbids Muslims to change their name and any form of identification. If they change their religion, the punishment is death. Islam supposedly teaches tolerance and Pakistani government boasts of being a democratic government, but when it comes to apostasy, the justice, tolerance, and freedom are seldom seen.

Mr. HM was a Taliban imam in a local mosque in the Swat area. He was trained to jihad i.e., war against the infidels. HM was brainwashed since his childhood that Christians are infidels and killing them would be rewarded by seventy-two virgins in the paradise. One morning when he finished his usual Friday sermon, he witnessed the horrific prosecution of a boy and a girl who were accused of meeting together before their marriage. As per the judgment, these two youngsters received lashes and were tortured. After the beating, the girl was raped by the three Taliban judges and killed.

HM tried to intervene and save her, and he asked the judges to justify their behavior according to Islam. They told him to shut up or he would be killed too. This incident shook HM, as he was the father of five daughters. He thought the girl killed by these judges could have easily been his own daughter. He questioned his faith, left the mosque, and was met by our coworker in the area. HM was offered a Bible and Christian booklets. After reading these he contacted our local worker, who later made contact with me. HM studied for one year and accepted Jesus as his Savior. Now his wife, five daughters, and three sons have also accepted Christ.

Another Pashtun young man—AA—has also come to Christ. AA comes from a highly influential political family in the northern area. He received a Bible from us during our refugee work near him. After reading the Bible and seeing our work, he was touched and gave his life to Christ. Because of his conversion his own father tortured him, almost killing AA with his own gun. AA ran for his life.

After a few months, he was lured back to his home and poisoned by his father. He was taken to the local hospital and survived. Then he was kidnapped by his father's hired mercenaries. He was tortured and asked to give up his Christian faith, but he refused. At the moment, he is in hiding. The last time I spoke with him, he told me that his persecution is nothing compared to what he has witnessed. He was resolute in his belief and recited Philippians 1:21, "For to me to live is Christ, and to die is gain."

Through every trial and hardship, Pakistani believers have emerged stronger in faith. Persecution also brought many seekers and converts, thus causing the Church to grow in ways that would not have been possible if there had not been persecution.

A WORD OF HOPE AND ENCOURAGEMENT FOR THE AMERICAN CHURCH

Today American society is embracing same-sex marriages, as reflected by the recent Supreme Court rulings.[11] The state of Colorado has legalized the use of marijuana.[12] There is a growing majority of the younger population who affiliate themselves as atheists, agnostics, and nihilists.[13] Most students at the Ivy League campuses believe premarital sex and living as common-law partners is fine with their moral standards.

With an estimated 1.1 million abortions annually,[14] the whole moral fabric of American society is in jeopardy. From parents fighting to keep the creation curriculum in the public schools[15] to an ever-increasing intellectual academia that challenges the core tenets of Christian doctrine, the American church faces an uphill task. Mainstream media, pop culture, the scientific community, and the capitalistic rat race are trying to tear down the already decaying churches. How can believers stay strong in the midst of an evolving assault on the American church from the legislative, judicial, and executive branches?

I am reminded of Psalm 126 where the psalmist says, "those who sow in tears shall reap with shouts of joy" (v. 5). Christians all over the world are sowing the seeds of the Gospel in very challenging and painful circumstances. This is not new. Our history is full of Christians who suffered for their faith.

Do not be discouraged when you are prohibited from proclaiming your faith in public. Do not be dejected when you become a social outcast because you choose to obey God. Do not be frustrated when you are mocked for professing your religious beliefs. Take heart when you are singled out at your workplace or denied a promotion because of your biblical worldview. Rejoice when you face social, political, and economic hardships because of your Savior, the Lord Jesus Christ.

Despite hostile circumstances, the hand of the Lord has led to the immense growth of my work at Grace Ministries. The slowly decaying congregations have been revived into a zealous part of the body of Christ. More than ten thousand believers around the city of

Faisalabad, Punjab, have found eternal hope in the Lord. Currently, Grace Ministries is running a theological seminary where more than twenty young men and women are being equipped to face persecution and turn discrimination into harvest.

My spouse is running a children's Sunday school program and preparing young Daniels and Esthers for tomorrow. Whenever we were surrounded by temptations, trials, and tribulations, we were reminded by God that He will never forsake us. *He* is in charge of His universe. His plan and calendar is bigger and better than ours. *God has, is, and will make a way when there seems to be no way.*

> **TO ALL THOSE who devoted their lives to a greater, purer, and holier cause: we salute you.**

Ultimately, I believe the Word of God is the greatest comfort for people who suffer in pain. Nothing can substitute for the power of the Word of God as it is shared. Luke 14:27 reminds us about carrying our cross and following *Him.* The Lord is calling Christians in America to carry their crosses and follow Him. The road ahead may not be easy, but with the Lord's grace, we will keep moving on.[16] I leave you with comforting words from Romans 8:35–39:

> Who shall separate us from the love of Christ? Shall tribulation, or distress, or persecution, or famine, or nakedness, or danger, or sword? As it is written, "For your sake we are being killed all the day long; we are regarded as sheep to be slaughtered." No, in all these things we are more than conquerors through him who loved us. For I am sure that neither death nor life, nor angels nor rulers, nor things present nor things to come, nor powers, nor height nor depth, nor anything else in all creation, will be able to separate us from the love of God in Christ Jesus our Lord.

The purpose of this chapter is to pay tribute to all the great souls who are facing persecution on a daily basis. To all those who devoted their lives to a greater, purer, and holier cause: we salute you. This cause went beyond worldly desires and spread the Gospel to the four corners of the world—a cause that changed lives forever.

This chapter also remembers the sacrifices of our forefathers, who selflessly gave up their flesh to attain eternal life. The life stories shared here are to provide hope and encouragement for the American church, who will be experiencing persecution in the foreseeable future. Do not be discouraged by this narrow, thorny path. See it as an opportunity to do justice, love mercy, and walk humbly with your God.

10

THE HOPE
OF REVIVAL

O Lord, I have heard the report of you,
and your work, O Lord, do I fear.
In the midst of the years revive it.

HABAKKUK 3:2

Since I was raised in the Midwest far from either coast, and my ministry career kept me rooted here, I've always enjoyed my rare chances to sit on a sandy beach and watch the ebbs and flows of the ocean. One wave splashes happily onto the shore—straining to extend its watery arms as far as possible—only to be drawn back into the ocean and regather as another foamy wave pounds for shore. The rhythm is soothing, predictable, and—for me—fascinating.

The work of God through spiritual revivals has often been compared to the pattern of waves hitting a shoreline.[1] A powerful movement of God sweeps across the land, irresistibly altering human society and eternally changing the destiny of thousands. Then it dissipates like a wave retreating into the ocean. During the inevitable ebb following a revival, man returns to sinful patterns, society suffers, and the righteous beg God for a fresh influx of His Spirit. In God's grace and sovereignty another spiritual awakening arrests mankind, blowing forcefully across the country and bringing refreshment for the nation.

America seems to be in the low ebb between revivals. Her spiritual waves have receded, unveiling a propensity for ungodliness fueled by a dangerous cocktail of unprecedented affluence and biblical illiteracy. It's a modern retelling of the book of Judges where "everyone is doing what is right in their own eyes." When we think society cannot sink any lower, it does. Unsavory practices are discussed and approved which would have been unthinkable two decades ago.

We desperately need a fresh wave of God's Spirit to crash across America. To salvage this nation for our children and grandchildren and to save us from ourselves, we need revival. Not the so-called revival advertised on church billboards inviting us to scheduled meetings next Saturday. We need an unrelenting, nation-changing, awe-inspiring, church-filling movement of God.

Can it happen? Revival is God's work, and our God hasn't lost one ounce of His power. This is kid's stuff to Him. Will it happen? That's the key question. Considering I can barely find my car keys in the morning, I don't know if it will. But if we want God to bring revival to America, we should understand how these powerful spiritual movements occurred in the past.

WHAT IS "REVIVAL"?

In the academic discipline of church history, few subjects merit more spirited discussion than revivals and revivalism. All scholars admit the existence of revivals, but debates rage as to their source, purpose, and value.[2] We need a definition.

Harold J. Ockenga once defined revival as "A condition when men give primary interest and attention to the things of God above their livelihood, above their intellectual pursuits, and above their social interests. A terror of wrongdoing descends upon them. A passion for repentance seizes them. A desire for salvation characterizes them. Men go on a search for God."[3]

J. Edwin Orr—considered dean of this discipline—said a revival is a movement "marked by the outpouring of the Holy Spirit, resulting in the revival of the Church and the awakening of the masses, and the mobilization of believers for evangelism, teaching, and social change."[4]

WE DESPERATELY need a fresh wave of God's Spirit to crash across America.

However you frame the definition, it's important to clarify what revival is and isn't. Revival is a sovereign, gracious work of God where He chooses to quicken hearts and build His church. It isn't man's production or manipulations. Revival is the Spirit's movement leading to dramatic spiritual growth in God's people. It isn't the same as evangelism, though it always results in effective mass evangelism. To illustrate the relationship between revival and evangelism, picture revival as wind and evangelism as the tree branch bent by the wind. One is the cause, the other is the effect.

A BRIEF HISTORY OF AMERICAN REVIVALS

Since before America's founding, this land has been the scene of gracious visits from God through revival. Orr summarizes American revivalism into five Great Awakenings.[5]

1. The First Great Awakening (1725–75)

Birthed in the German Moravian movement, this revival started in New Jersey and swept across the New England colonies utilizing the powerful oratory skills of John Wesley and George Whitefield. Churches filled to capacity with attentive audiences. It's estimated that out of a population of 300,000 in New England, 30,000 new converts were added to the church in two years (1740–42).[6]

The revival made a significant social impact on higher education. Seeking to train more ministers, nine university colleges were established between 1740–70 and six of them (Princeton, Brown, Dartmouth, Pennsylvania, Columbia, and Rutgers) were a direct result of the Awakening.[7] The revival also planted the first seeds of abolitionism.

The First Great Awakening ended with the Revolutionary War, which shattered denominational cooperation and placed church groups on opposite sides of the political equation. But as President Calvin Coolidge once observed, "America was born in a Revival of Religion."

2. The Second Great Awakening (1792–1830)

Rapid moral decline followed the First Great Awakening. Orr writes, "Out of five million population, 300,000 were drunkards, 15,000 dying annually. Increased sexual license boosted illegitimacy and venereal disease. There was a surfeit of lawlessness and a multiplication of robberies."[8] Humanistic propaganda from the French Revolution took root on college campuses. A poll of Princeton students revealed only two believers in the entire student body, and other campuses saw students destroying Bibles and disrupting worship.[9]

The Second Awakening launched from a prayer movement in England and moved to Boston. By 1794, churches across America were making fervent intercession on the first Monday of every month. The resulting revival started in Massachusetts, and by 1798 had spread across New England to the frontier territories, bringing dramatic numbers to Christ. The secular colleges were reclaimed for Christ, led by Timothy Dwight, who became Yale's president in 1795.[10] New evangelical associations were formed including the American Bible Society, the American Tract Society, and several foreign missions organizations.

3. The Revival of 1830 (1830–42)

Unlike the moral slump that plagued America after the First Great Awakening, the Second Great Awakening had a nearly seamless transition into another outpouring of the Spirit in 1830. At the center was Charles G. Finney, a controversial historical figure.

Despite Finney, vast numbers converted to Christ. The Methodists reported a nearly one million member increase in just over a decade.[11] New believers worked feverishly for the welfare of society. Orr comments, "They promoted ardently the emancipation of the slaves, a protection of prisoners, a care of the sick, an improvement of working conditions, a safe-guarding of women and children, an extension of folk education, the founding of hospitals, asylums, orphanages, schools, high schools and colleges."[12] The revival's England branch founded the Young Men's Christian Association (YMCA), which would enter the United States in the 1850s.

4. The Revival of 1858 (1858–95)

The Revival of 1830 lasted twelve years and ended because of growing division over slavery, increased affluence, and disillusionment spawned by William Miller's faulty eschatology.[13]

A new spiritual revival began in an environment of fervent prayer. In February 1858, six thousand businessmen were gathering regularly in New York City for prayer. One thousand daily intercessors met for midday prayer in Pittsburgh. Five daily prayer meetings were held in Washington, D.C.[14]

When revival began sweeping the country—despite the Civil War's outbreak—evangelist Dwight L. Moody led thousands to faith in Christ. When the war ended, the Awakening spiraled to even greater heights, continuing to the mid-1890s and creating unparalleled expansion for churches. At the revival's peak fifty thousand people were saved every week.[15] *The Washington National Intelligencer* reported it was impossible to find an unsaved soul in many towns in the New England states.[16]

Because of this revival, Bible societies flourished in England and America. William Booth started the Salvation Army and Hudson

Taylor launched the very first faith mission, the China Inland Mission. Moody started the Moody Bible Institute in Chicago, and his remarkable harvest of intellectuals at Cambridge led to the Student Volunteer Movement which—in one year—saw three thousand students commit their lives to international missions. Over half a century, the Student Volunteer Movement enlisted more than twenty thousand students.[17]

5. The Awakening of 1904 (1904–40)

An early twentieth century revival, often called the Awakening of 1904, emerged from prayer cells "which seemed to arise spontaneously all over the world, combining into streams of expectation which became a flood of blessing."[18] An astounding revival swept across Wales in 1904–05, causing churches to overflow. Over a two-year period over one hundred thousand people came to salvation. The effect on Welsh society became legendary: "Drunkenness was immediately cut in half, and many taverns went bankrupt. Crime was so diminished that judges were presented with white gloves attesting that there were no causes of murder, assault, rape, or robbery to consider. Local police became unemployed in many districts."[19]

When the Awakening crossed to the States it rolled across the entire country. Atlantic City reported only fifty adults remained unconverted out of sixty thousand.[20] Every business and factory in Burlington, Iowa, closed to allow employees opportunity to attend prayer services. Denver's mayor declared a day of prayer. Two hundred stores in Portland, Oregon, signed agreements to close from 11 a.m. to 2 p.m. for prayer. Church membership in America increased overall by more than two million in five years.[21]

The revival finally reached an ebb through disillusionment with war and the economic struggles of the Great Depression. In the post–World War II era the spiritual decline became so pronounced Ockenga, then pastor of Park Street Church in Boston, proclaimed in a 1947 lectureship at Dallas Theological Seminary,

> We realize that we are in the ebb-tide of revival waves. Darkness has engulfed our age. Sin, fear, hate, doubt, distrust, and despair characterize the dominant mood of this day. Men's hearts are failing them for fear of things that are coming upon the earth. The moral collapse of this hour is universal . . . Mass bombings, mass transferals of population, mass planned starvation, are evidences of the fact that all nations, including the United States, have abandoned the Christian principles of civilization. Individuals have cast Christian ethics out the window so that immorality is rampant.[22]

Ebb and flow. For over two centuries America experienced refreshing waves of God's Spirit sweeping the country—and the dark spiritual malaise which inevitably follows.

WHAT HAPPENS IN REVIVAL

What can we learn from America's history of revivals? While recognizing they aren't humanly engineered but sovereignly given by God as He fulfills His eternal purposes, there are commonalities to a genuine, reviving work of the Spirit. Ockenga, in his lectures after extensive research, identified the following characteristics of revival.[23]

Spiritual Progress Is Never Steady

It moves forward and falls back. There are periods of intense spiritual interest followed by noticeable disinterest. The book of Judges shows this aggravating interchange: Israel cries to God for deliverance from their oppressors. God graciously sends a judge to rescue them, causing them to rejoice. They follow God for a while, but then the cycle repeats itself and they fall into sin. Ebb and flow. Forward and back. Knowing the human condition, we shouldn't expect anything different. Spiritual progress is never steady and constant.

Revivals Are Periodic but Not Predictable

History shows a periodic pattern to America's revivals. After a number of years, for reasons only known to God, He sends spiritual revival. The pattern isn't predictable because it remains within God's will, but historical evidence suggests—notwithstanding the wild card of human behavior—we can expect revival again someday.

Revivals Follow Pitiful Seasons in the Church

When a revival diminishes, spiritual lethargy regains its grip on human hearts. Worldliness takes a prominent role, and the pursuit of God characterizing revival is a distant memory. Evangelism is neglected; interest in Bible study disappears. The spiritual landscape becomes as dry as the desert. In the midst of deadness, a faint cry lifts to God as a soul longs for better days. Ockenga calls this "the first harbinger of revival."[24]

A Leader Emerges Who Incarnates the Revival Message

Like Israel's judges, God raises a key leader who possesses the gifts and character to personify the revival. It could be a Whitefield, Wesley, or Moody. By divine design, this leader is "more sensitive to the longings of men, the ideas of his day" and "the whisperings of the Spirit."[25]

Revival Rolls Irresistibly over the Land

Fresh spiritual energy emerges, and the weary souls spring up in new life. Just as men cannot turn back an approaching storm, neither can people resist the Spirit's movement. Sorrow overwhelms them. They confess sin, leading to outbursts of joy as men and women find forgiveness and grace. Hope again permeates the land, and those who find Christ take every opportunity to tell others the good news.

The Nation Is Transformed for Good

While individual lives are eternally transformed through their decisions for Christ, America's corporate life is also profoundly changed. Ockenga writes, "The result of a revival is always a higher ethical standard through the changed lives of the people."[26]

IN THE MIDST of deadness, a faint cry lifts to God as a soul longs for better days.

The church returns to its divine calling and message. The cross becomes central. Educational reform occurs, corruption is discarded, and governmental leaders are held to righteous standards. It's not a stretch to say that most of America's societal advancements came in the middle of and through revival.

Can this happen again? Can revival return to America? We're clearly in the ebb tide now, as witnessed in the dramatic cultural trajectory of abandoning God's Word. It's possible the ebb will subside and a wave will build again towards revival.

WHAT SPARKS REVIVAL

Based on observed revival history and a biblical knowledge on how God brings blessing to a land, there are requirements we must meet if we long for revival. While meeting these prerequisites doesn't obligate God to give us a fresh effusion of His Spirit, we can confidently state that unless we prepare ourselves, the likelihood of revival seems remote. Four requirements seem evident.

Humble Confession

In the ebb tide, sin gains the dominant hand. Perversity and unrighteousness can become so ingrained in our culture that we lose perspective. We don't recognize how far we've slipped because the slope has been gradual. As we saw in chapter 3 regarding cultural change, there's an integration process that occurs once the change has been formally incorporated into law. This integration masks reality for us. One falling domino leads to another. Without a stake in the ground, we unwittingly adopt cultural mores far from our biblical roots.

Therefore, individual confession is necessary as God reveals our sin to us. More importantly, corporate confession is required. The church—as a local gathering of believers, and the universal church—as the people of God, must humble ourselves and admit we failed as His representatives on earth. We're called to be salt and light but, as Christ says in Matthew 5:13, "If salt has lost its taste, how shall its saltiness be restored? It is no longer good for anything except to be thrown out and trampled under people's feet."

> **PERVERSITY and unrighteousness can become so ingrained in our culture that we lose perspective.**

How does salt regain its saltiness? Through humble confession. Ockenga writes, "We must experience shame and sorrow for our sins, over our lack of love to Christ, over our deflection from pursuit of revealed objectives, over our worldly spirit, over bitter acrimony, over dulled consciences. We must confess that we have been preoccupied with things which have shut out our enthusiasm for the Lord's work."[27]

Fervent Prayer

Our greatest privilege as God's children is access to the throne of grace. As His children, God grants us the freedom to come into His presence as often as we desire and express our twisted struggles, deepest pain, inner yearnings, and heartfelt dreams. Assuming we come through the blood of the Lamb and with clean hands, God is always ready to listen. And if our requests are consistent with His sovereign will, He'll respond.

Jesus reminds us of the great privilege of prayer in Matthew 7.

Ask, and it will be given to you; seek and you will find; knock and it will be opened to you. For everyone who asks receives, and the one who seeks finds, and to the one who knocks it will be opened. Or which one of you, if his son asks him for bread, will give him a stone? Or if he asks for a fish, will give him a serpent? If you then, who are evil, know how to give good gifts to your children, how much more will your Father who is in heaven give good things to those who ask him! (vv. 7–11)

Believers who long for revival to blow fresh in America must ask God for it. While God may have eternal purposes for our nation's spiritual demise—purposes that remain hidden from us (Rom. 11:33)—based on His Word we know He desires justice and righteousness in all lands (Mic. 6:8). This proper moral and spiritual orientation will come not through an altered political process but through a spiritual revival. Like a mighty wind, it needs to sweep across the country and reset the thinking and actions of everyone from Wall Street to Main Street.

We must pray fervently for revival. James 5:16 reminds us, "The prayer of a righteous person has great power as it is working." As we observed in our brief history of the various awakenings, revivals have always been preceded by prayer. It can start with a handful of people, but as God moves in hearts—as we saw in previous examples— others will be compelled to interrupt their lives and join in seeking His face, begging Him to bring spiritual refreshment to America.

There are hints this is beginning. A prayer movement called One-Cry (www.onecry.com) wants to unite believers to ask God to revive the church and transform our nation. If we want revival, hitting our knees in fervent prayer is required.

Vibrant Faith

Faith is the third prerequisite if we yearn to see revival. This faith isn't the faith we exercise for eternal salvation; it's faith that believes God can bring revival. It's faith that humbly realizes we cannot bring a soul-shaking, culture-changing awakening by ourselves. Revival must be sourced in God's power as the Creator of the universe. A vibrant faith believes God will do this.

Jesus says God intently looks for such faith. He told His disciples, "Truly, I say to you, if you have faith like a grain of mustard seed, you will say to this mountain, 'Move from here to there' and it will move, and nothing will be impossible for you" (Matt. 17:20). The mustard seed is among the smallest seeds in Israel. That's all the faith that's needed because it's not *us* moving the mountain but the *object* of our faith moving it—God Himself.

Our faith can be the size of a mustard seed, but it cannot be compromised by doubt. James cautions us when he says, "But let him ask in faith, with no doubting, for the one who doubts is like a wave of the sea that is driven and tossed by the wind. For that person must not suppose that he will receive anything from the Lord; he is a double-minded man, unstable in all his ways" (James 1:6–8). *Double-minded* means we vacillate between belief and unbelief. One day we believe God can bring revival, the next we doubt.

> **A FRESH VISIT from God requires an ever-increasing multitude who firmly believes *God will do this*.**

Revival won't be ushered in by compromised faith. A fresh visit from God requires an ever-increasing multitude who firmly believe God *will do this*.

Bold Evangelism

When we're at an ebb tide, our natural tendency is timidity in proclaiming the gospel. The environment is hostile and few seem interested, so we muffle our voices. The church shows disinterest in evangelism, moving its scarce resources to more productive activities.

But every American spiritual revival was linked with bold, mass-evangelism campaigns. Finney, Moody, and Billy Sunday led the way, and other less-familiar names—such as Wilbur Chapman—added to the steady diet of gospel preaching. Evangelism isn't the *essence of* revival, but it's an unmistakable *requirement for* revival. Ockenga says, "Only such a corporate movement can roll back the tides of sin which are engulfing society today. Individual soul-winning is wonderful, but it is not enough. Hence we must have great campaigns 'that the world may believe.' "[28]

Paul expressed the needed attitude in Romans 1:16: "For I am not ashamed of the gospel, for it is the power of God for salvation to everyone who believes, to the Jew first and also to the Greek."

"NOW IS THE TIME"

Will God bring a new breath of His Spirit to America and rein in the sin and corruption, reshaping our culture to reflect righteousness? If we humbly confess, fervently pray, vibrantly believe, and boldly evangelize, will revival come? Only our sovereign God knows, but I am encouraged by how God answered His people the last time we cried to Him.

As I described earlier, it was an ebb time after World War II. When Ockenga stood before the students and faculty at Dallas Seminary in 1947, he lamented our country's desperate state of affairs. In a later lecture he said, "Ours is a time of disinterested persons. A great mass of men are utterly indifferent to the claims of God upon their lives. They live as though there were no church. Life for them is totally secular and passes by everything spiritual."[29] His words would accurately describe today's society almost seventy years later. Ockenga, along with others, sought God's face, praying for revival. Did it come?

Oh yes—it came. Starting two years later in 1949, America experienced a resurgence often referred to in history books as the Eisenhower revival, as it spanned Dwight Eisenhower's years in the White House. The movement's initial energy came with the establishment of a new, Saturday-night evangelistic youth ministry in Chicago called Youth for Christ.[30]

Finding success reaching youth in Chicago, the rallies spread to other major cities and utilized evangelistic preachers such as Torrey Johnson, Jack Wyrtzen, Chuck Templeton, Merv Rosell, and Billy Graham. The floodgates of revival soon opened. Rosell writes, "The 'mercy drops' of revival had been falling throughout the 1940s, but 1949–50 brought a veritable downpour of spiritual awakening."[31]

The downpour started with a Billy Graham evangelistic crusade in Los Angeles, slated for twenty-two nights starting September 25, 1949. Thirty-year-old Graham was the president of Northwestern College in Minneapolis and known as a youth speaker who held campaigns in smaller cities. In Los Angeles—surprising everyone but the Lord—the meetings extended far past their original schedule, totaling eight weeks and seventy-two meetings with over three thousand people trusting Christ.[32]

Ockenga sensed the winds of revival blowing and invited Graham to Boston to speak at a youth rally in the six-thousand-seat Mechanics Hall on New Year's Eve, 1949. No one anticipated the outcome. Mechanics Hall was packed—every seat full and hundreds more turned away. The four-hour meeting made the front page of Sunday's edition of the *Boston Post*, which provided a detailed report listing all the main participants.[33] Ockenga proclaimed, "The hour of revival has struck. New England is ripe for evangelism. The same yearning which is seen over the land is experienced here. Yesterday is gone. Tomorrow is uncertain, we only have today. Now is the time. Let us redeem it. Let us use it."[34]

It had been two centuries since New England experienced revival, but it came. What later was known as the New England Mid-Century Revival spread from Boston and touched all the major cities of the New England states. Graham returned to Boston for a short campaign in April 1950, which concluded with a Sunday afternoon service attended by fifty thousand.[35]

The marks of a revival were evident: scores of prayer meetings were held, churches were quickened, and people were saved. It spread to other parts of America as Graham and other evangelists criss-crossed the country. The peak came in 1957 during a sixteen-week crusade Graham held in New York City. Over two million people attended the meetings, and nearly one hundred thousand indicated decisions for Christ in person or via the telecasts.[36]

After a decade, the revival ended. Most historians consider 1960 the conclusion of the Eisenhower revival. The ebb in the tide returned as changing sexual mores, a growing drug culture, and increasing violence washed over American society. The same ebb continues today. The next wave of revival hasn't yet splashed on American soil. We've had over fifty years since the last Great Awakening. We're desperately parched.

Will it come? We have hope. Os Guinness writes,

We wait for God's answer, but as we wait, we work. We may be in the dark about our times, but we are not in the dark about God. Whatever the future holds, we are walking in the light with our Lord, so followers of Jesus must have the courage and the faith to work for a new renaissance in our time. So let there be no fear, nor alarmism, nor despondency, nor nostalgia. Instead, let us look up and so act with faith as to say with our prayers as with our lives, 'Let a thousand flowers bloom!' And let us care nothing for any fashionable talk of legacy, but leave the outcome of our enterprise to God and to history.[37]

If God graciously visits this land in a powerful way, the current cultural trends will be immediately arrested, biblical values will return, and the threat of persecution will disappear. And you won't need this book.

May we each fervently pray to that end.

AFTERWORD

Who shall separate us from the love of Christ?
Shall tribulation, or distress, or persecution,
or famine, or nakedness, or danger, or sword?

———

ROMANS 8:35

The future of America has yet to be etched in history. Since our nation's birth through a revolt against the British Empire over two hundred years ago, the United States has been a country that values and protects religious freedom. This value, reflecting biblical principles, contributed significantly to our country's greatness and provided the environment for Americans to lead the world in most Christian enterprises—including printing Bibles and sending missionaries.

As we have seen, our culture is in the midst of a radical makeover. Religious freedom is eroding as our postmodern society races toward a philosophical embrace of relativism and tolerance. The decrease in religious freedom inevitably brings a sharp increase in religious persecution.

The first examples of hostile opposition to Christians, unlike anything we've seen in the past, are starting to bubble to the surface. The current trends show no sign of abating—only accelerating as the generational shift continues. Unless the hearts of Americans are gripped and changed through another Great Awakening, believers can expect antagonism—with its attendant physical, emotional, and financial effects—to steadily increase.

Followers of Jesus all over the world are well-versed in persecution. They've suffered, persevered, and witnessed personal and corporate spiritual fruit which—to this point—remain elusive in America. They know the cost of taking up the cross of Christ. They see the spiritual purity forged when heat is raised against the church. It's a level of discipleship on its way to American believers.

WHAT TO DO BEFORE THE ATTACKS COME

For many of us, the persecution described in this book can seem like an approaching storm forecast by our local weather service. We believe it is coming, and we see the dark clouds forming, but we haven't experienced a change in our weather yet. If so, how should we spiritually prepare for what appears inevitable?

First, *be watchful.* If a storm is brewing, we always need to keep one eye on the clouds. Jesus told His disciples, "Stay dressed for action and keep your lamps burning" (Luke 12:35). The change in our cultural climate may not be uniform in all locations. Some believers may experience more and greater repercussions than others. The key is to stay alert and keep watching so that we are not caught unaware.

Second, *be faithful.* Watching the storm clouds forming must not stop us from continuing to keep our hand to the plow and stay faithful in the tasks God has given to us in this life. Prayer, diligence, evangelism, and discipleship are needed more than ever today if the environment around us is going to become more hostile.

> **THE KEY is to stay alert and keep watching so that we are not caught unaware.**

Finally, *be prudent.* Some of our accustomed creaturely comforts may be stripped from us in the near future. We may be forced to live with less, due to the economic persecution we face. If so, prudence calls for an attitude adjustment now to such physical comforts. While enjoyable, they are not necessary to a faithful and fruitful life. It is noteworthy that Jesus commanded His disciples to take with them only minimal supplies when they were sent out to minister to a hostile world (Luke 9:3).

WHAT TO DO WHEN THE ATTACKS COME

Without experience, none of us know how we'll respond when we first encounter persecution. We don't know what we'll do when the verbal attack comes, our job is threatened, or the police arrive at our doorstep. As we consider our response at that moment, the Bible gives us three options.

Flee

The first option the Bible gives us when facing persecution is to *flee from it*. Sometimes, the appropriate response is to remove yourself from the hostile situation.

Paul did this in Acts 9 after his Damascus conversion. He regains his sight through Ananias and begins to speak boldly about Jesus to the Jews in the synagogue. When the religious leaders realized they couldn't effectively answer Paul's arguments (and wanting to silence the defector), they plot to kill him. Had Paul remained in Damascus debating the Jews, his ministry might have been snuffed out before it extended beyond the city gates.

Due to the revelation God gave him of his future ministry before kings and Gentiles (Acts 9:15; Gal. 1:16), Paul knew martyrdom in Damascus wasn't God's will for him. So he sought an opportunity to escape. It wasn't possible to leave through the gates because the Jews were watching for him. His only available route came in a basket lowered through an opening in the wall (9:25; cf. 2 Cor.

11:32–33). He escaped, and arrived safely at the community of believers in Jerusalem.

Paul flees from persecution a second time in Acts 14 when he's in Iconium on his first missionary journey. With Barnabas, Paul enters the Jewish synagogue and proclaims Christ. Many Jews and Greeks believe. The two remain in Iconium for a period of weeks speaking boldly, performing miracles, and establishing the new church.

However, hostile Jews once again plot against him. Building a coalition of Gentiles and city leaders, the Jews hatch a plan to physically assault the two missionaries and stone them (v. 5). When Paul and Barnabas discover the plot, they quickly leave town, continuing their ministry in Lystra and Derbe (v. 6). We assume the Holy Spirit prompted their decision to flee.

Jesus also withdrew when plots were formed against Him. In Matthew 12, after Jesus and His disciples violated Pharisaic law concerning the Sabbath, the religious leaders "conspired against him, how to destroy him" (v. 14). Jesus knew His time hadn't yet come. Aware of their plan to kill Him, He left that region (v. 15).

Jesus gave His disciples freedom to flee persecution before He sent them out into ministry. After warning them they would be hated (Matt. 10:22) He says, "When they persecute you in one town, flee to the next, for truly I say to you, you will not have gone through all the towns of Israel before the Son of Man comes" (v. 23).

Fleeing persecution is a viable option if our mission is in jeopardy. It's not an acceptable option if we're avoiding pain, because persecution is integral to following Jesus and a powerful way God shapes us into Christ's image.

This is one reason God tells us to ask for wisdom in persecution (James 1:5). If we ask God for understanding when we face trials, the Holy Spirit will confirm if our mission will be compromised and we need to escape.

Defend Ourselves

A second biblical option when we encounter persecution is to *defend ourselves*. This doesn't mean we become pugilistic and pummel our opponents with our fists. Nor does it mean we empty a magazine from an automatic weapon. Such a physical fight contradicts the "turn the other cheek" principle of Matthew 5:39, violates Paul's command to not seek vengeance (Rom. 12:19), and disagrees with Christ's example in 1 Peter 2:23 teaching against retaliation.

Instead, this option allows us to *legally* defend ourselves. It's sometimes appropriate to defend ourselves against accusers in a court of law. Paul often defended himself as a Roman citizen. In Philippi Paul and Silas were illegally beaten with rods and thrown into prison without the benefit of a fair trial (Acts 16:22–24). When God freed them through an earthquake in the middle of the night, the magistrates ordered the police to let them go.

We expect Paul, having escaped yet another brush with death, would gladly accept the offer. He chooses instead to defend his rights. He responds to the police, "They have beaten us publicly, uncondemned, men who are Roman citizens, and have thrown us into prison; and do they now throw us out secretly? No! Let them come themselves and take us out" (v. 37). The Philippi magistrates come to the prison and personally apologize.

Paul engaged in a longer, more involved defense of his actions when arrested in the temple after his third missionary journey. He first invoked his rights when a Roman tribune ordered Paul be flogged to force him to say why the Jewish religious leaders were against him (Acts 22:24). As they raised their whips to beat him Paul asked the centurion, "Is it lawful for you to flog a man who is a Roman citizen and uncondemned?" (v. 25). Shocked, the centurion immediately halted the illegal punishment.

Paul's legal proceedings continue through the rest of Acts. He appears before Felix in Caesarea (chapter 24), Festus in Jerusalem (chapter 25), King Agrippa in Jerusalem (25:13–26:32), and successfully makes an appeal to plead his case in Rome before Caesar himself (chapters 27–28). This legal defense was missional, as Paul had a divine calling to represent Christ before the Gentiles and kings (Acts 9:15). His elongated defense enabled Paul to fulfill it.

At times it's appropriate to defend our rights in court. That's what the Green family—owners of Hobby Lobby—did before the Supreme Court, challenging the ACA's contraception mandate. Though our religious freedoms are eroding, as citizens of the United States we should require enforcement of our rights and protections.

We might be hesitant to pursue legal action due to unfamiliarity with our options or limited resources. Fortunately, there are legal organizations who exist to counsel and represent believers on religious freedom issues. Both the National Center for Life and Liberty (www.ncll.org) and the Alliance Defending Freedom (www.alliancedefendingfreedom.org) are worth considering if you choose to legally defend yourself.

Stand Firm

A third biblical option when we face persecution is to *stand firm*. This demands we endure the trial and not fight to get out from underneath it. In most cases, if a legal issue isn't involved, this is God's will for our lives.

While in rare situations Paul fled from persecution, most of the time he didn't. He left Iconium, but was stoned in Lystra (Acts 14:19) and even went back into the city when he was revived. He was flogged in Philippi and locked in prison (Acts 16:23–24). He faced a mob in Thessalonica (Acts 17:4–7) and started a riot in the streets of Ephesus (Acts 19). He suffered a long litany of wounds through standing firm in persecution (e.g., 2 Cor. 11:23–27).

When Christ knew it wasn't time for His suffering, He withdrew from hostile crowds. But when His time came, He willingly endured the cross and suffered the shame. Jesus' command to His disciples to remain in Jerusalem (Acts 1:4) awaiting the Holy Spirit on Pentecost was also a call to stand firm and endure. In the aftermath of the crucifixion and resurrection, Jerusalem was extremely hostile. While the disciples likely would've preferred retreating to the safety of Galilee, Jesus required them to stand firm.

In most situations this is our call. God's plan usually calls for us to not flee from hostility but be strong through it.

Fear Not

While we have the biblical options of fleeing, defending ourselves, and standing firm when we encounter persecution, fear isn't an option. We may have a natural fear of the physical and emotional pain we could suffer if we're punished, but the Bible says we're not to be afraid of our enemies.

Jesus makes this clear to His disciples. After telling them He's sending them out as sheep in the midst of wolves (Matt. 10:16), Jesus says, "So have no fear of them . . . do not fear those who kill the body but cannot kill the soul. Rather fear him who can destroy both soul and body in hell" (vv. 26, 28). In short, He says fear God—not man.

Why can't we be afraid of our enemies? Because their power is limited to the physical realm. Our opponents may end our physical lives, but that's the most they can do. They cannot end our spiritual lives, so man shouldn't be feared. Osborne writes, "If all a person can do is destroy your mortal body, that is nothing to fear. The most important part of a person, the soul, will live on."[1]

In contrast, God is to be feared because He has authority over both our temporal body and our eternal soul. Referring to Matthew 10:26–28, Dietrich Bonhoeffer wrote:

The danger lies not in the judgment of men, but in the judgment of God, not in the death of the body, but in the eternal destruction of body and soul. Those who are still afraid of men have no fear of God, and those who have fear of God have ceased to be afraid of men.[2]

Peter echoes this in 1 Peter 3:14–15: "But even if you should suffer for righteousness' sake, you will be blessed. Have no fear of them, nor be troubled, but in your hearts honor Christ the Lord as holy." When we fear others we give them control over our lives. We yield to them as our lords. But our enemies are not in control—God is. He and He alone is to be feared—not man.

WHAT IF WE FAIL?

Not knowing what awaits us, we can worry about failure. What if we fail miserably in the face of persecution? What if we dishonor our Lord in our actions and attitudes despite our best intentions?

None of us want to fail, but at some point it's inevitable. We remain deeply flawed creatures and, as Jesus explained in the garden of Gethsemane just moments from their supreme hour of testing, "the spirit indeed is willing, but the flesh is weak" (Matt. 26:41).

The disciples failed miserably. Peter boasted in the upper room that "though they all fall away because of you, I will never fall away" (Matt. 26:33). Hours later when soldiers came with swords and torches to arrest Jesus, Peter deserted Christ with everyone else. Jesus was left alone to face His oppressors.

Peter's failure didn't end with his flight from Gethsemane. It grew through his three-fold denial of Christ when challenged by a servant girl. "You know Jesus?" "Nope!" Three pitches in the middle of the strike zone; three whiffs by Peter. The crow of the rooster sealed the worst night of his life.

We'll have days like that. We'll have ugly, forgettable moments when we fail. Instead of displaying graciousness, we'll get angry. Instead of blessing our enemies, we'll curse them. Instead of turning the other cheek, we'll retaliate. Count on it.

What should we do when we fail our Lord? Get up. Get back up, confess our failure, and stay in the race knowing God wants to restore us and use us. He didn't leave Peter in the dumps, and He won't leave us there either.

Peter reminds us what God will do for us—just as He did for him—when he writes, "After you have suffered a little while, the God of all grace, who has called you to his eternal glory in Christ, will himself restore, confirm, strengthen, and establish you" (1 Pet. 5:10).

WHAT SHOULD we do when we fail our Lord? Get up.

When failure comes (as it will), note the verbs in the above verse. God Himself will "restore" (fix what is broken), "confirm" (make firm), "strengthen" (provide new support), and "establish" (supply a buttress to stabilize) us. This is a promise from our gracious God, and He personally will do this. When failure comes, get back up again, dust yourself off, and keep running.

The rest of our stories are yet to be written. Persecution provides us with the valuable opportunity to take our commitment to Christ to a new level. Persecution gives us the chance to demonstrate to a watching and hostile world what true discipleship looks like. Persecution supplies the life-shaping tools God skillfully uses to mold us into Christ's image. It's the next chapter in our stories.

How do you want your story to end?

Now's the time to prepare.

NOTES

Introduction

1. Todd Starnes, "The city of Houston demands pastors turn over sermons," *Fox News*, October 14, 2014, accessed November 2, 2014, http://www.foxnews.com/opinion/2014/10/14/city-houston-demands-pastors-turn-over-sermons/.

2. Alexis de Tocqueville, a French aristocrat and writer who both studied and wrote about American democracy, is an example. He said, "The Americans combine the notions of Christianity and of liberty so intimately in their minds that it is impossible to make them conceive the one without the other."

3. Glenn Penner, *In the Shadow of the Cross: A Biblical Theology of Persecution and Discipleship* (Bartlesville, OK: Living Sacrifice Books, 2004), 17.

4. John S. Dickerson, *The Great Evangelical Recession: Six Factors That Will Crash the American Church . . . and How to Prepare* (Grand Rapids: Baker, 2013), 41.

5. Ibid. Dickerson's second chapter, "Hated," should be required reading for every evangelical leader in America.

6. Erwin W. Lutzer, *Where Do We Go From Here? Hope and Direction in Our Present Crisis* (Chicago: Moody, 2013), 5.

7. Billy Graham, *Storm Warning: Whether Global Recession, Terrorist Threats, or Devastating Natural Disasters, These Ominous Shadows Must Bring Us Back to the Gospel* (Nashville: Thomas Nelson, 2010), Kindle edition locations 132 and 141.

8. Geoffrey W. Bromiley, "Persecute; Persecution," in *The International Standard Bible Encyclopedia*, vol. 3, ed. Geoffrey W. Bromiley (Grand Rapids: Eerdmans, 1986), 771.

9. "Inside the Persecution Numbers," *Christianity Today*, March 2014, 14.

10. Penner, *In the Shadow of the Cross*, 169.

Chapter 1: Awakening to a Different World

1. I use the word *lost* in relative—not absolute—terms. God is still sovereign and has the final word on the destiny of any nation. In the last chapter, I'll explore what could happen if revival were to sweep the land. But barring a powerful spiritual awakening, my conclusion is correct: we have lost the cultural war. A recent survey conducted by LifeWay Research confirms this (February 20, 2014, accessed July 18, 2014, http://www.lifewayresearch.com/2014/02/20/lifeway-research-pastors-believe-religious-liberty-on-decline-in-u-s).

2. Ross Douthat, "The Terms of Our Surrender," *New York Times*, March 1, 2014, accessed May 1, 2014, http://www.nytimes.com/2014/03/02/opinion/sunday/the-terms-of-our-surrender.html.

3. Oliver Thomas, "Restricting Religion Will Not Unite Us," *USA Today*, March 18, 2014, 7A.

4. Douthat, "The Terms of Our Surrender."

5. Erick Erickson, "You Will Be Made to Care," *RedState*, December 9, 2013, accessed July 18, 2014, http://www.redstate.com/2013/12/09/you-will-be-made-to-care-3.

6. I am referring to the initial foray into this arena by Matthew Vines titled *God and the Gay Christian* (Portland: Convergent Books, 2014). Notable scholars have soundly refuted his arguments, so I will not discuss them here. I expect other similar works seeking to create questions about the biblical view of marriage will emerge in the near future.

7. A good summary of the 1996 DOMA law can be found at http://thomas.loc.gov/cgi-bin/bdquery/z?d104:HR03396:@@@D&summ2=m& (accessed July 18, 2014).

8. Bill Clinton, "It's time to overturn DOMA," *Washington Post*, March 7, 2013, accessed July 18, 2014, http://www.washingtonpost.com/opinions/bill-clinton-its-time-to-overturn-doma/2013/03/07/fc184408-8747-11e2-98a3-b3db6b9ac586_story.html.

9. Michael O'Brien, "Clintons Hail DOMA Ruling," *NBC News*, June 26, 2013, accessed July 18, 2014, http://nbcpolitics.nbcnews.com/_news/2013/06/26/19156331-clintons-hail-doma-ruling.

10. David G. Savage, "Court's 'historic' move in gay marriage battle," *Chicago Tribune*, October 7, 2014.

11. William Saletan, "Purge the Bigots," *Slate*, April 4, 2014, accessed July 18, 2014, http://www.slate.com/articles/news_and_politics/frame_game/2014/04/brendan_eich_quits_mozilla_let_s_purge_all_the_antigay_donors_to_prop_8.html.

12. Ibid.

13. Hal Dardick, "Alderman to Chick-fil-A: No Deal," *Chicago Tribune*, June 25, 2012, accessed July 18, 2014, http://articles.chicagotribune.com/2012-07-25/news/ct-met-chicago-chick-fil-a-20120725_1_1st-ward-gay-marriage-ward-alderman.

14. Ibid.

15. Todd Starnes, *God Less America: Real Stories from the Front Lines of the Attack on Traditional Values* (Lake Mary, FL: Charisma House, 2014), 64.

16. Erwin W. Lutzer, *Where Do We Go From Here? Hope and Direction in Our Present Crisis* (Chicago: Moody, 2013), 39.

17. Albert Mohler, "God, the Gospel, and the Gay Challenge—A Response to Matthew Vines," *AlbertMohler.com*, April 22, 2014, accessed July 18, 2014, http://www.albertmohler.com/2014/04/22/god-the-gospel-and-the-gay-challenge-a-response-to-matthew-vines.

18. Emma Green, "The U.S. Puts 'Moderate' Restrictions on Religious Freedom," *The Atlantic*, January 28, 2014, accessed July 18, 2014, http://www.theatlantic.com/national/archive/2014/01/

the-us-puts-moderate-restrictions-on-religious-freedom/283331.

19. Mike Florio, "NFL had begun considering alternatives to Arizona for Super Bowl XLIX," *NBC Sports*, February 27, 2014, accessed July 18, 2014, http://profootballtalk.nbcsports.com/2014/02/27/ nfl-had-begun-considering-alternatives-to-arizona-for-super-bowl-xlix.

20. Thomas Black and Jennifer Oldham, "Delta joins Apple in Opposing Arizona Anti-Gay Measure," *Business Week*, February 26, 2014, accessed July 18, 2014, http://www.businessweek.com/news/2014-02-26/ delta-joining-apple-as-opposition-to-anti-gay-law-goes-national.

21. Catherine E. Schoichet and Halimah Abdullah, "Arizona Gov. Jan Brewer vetoes controversial anti-gay bill, SB 1062," *CNN Politics*, February 26, 2014, accessed July 18, 2014, http://www.cnn.com/2014/02/26/politics/ arizona-brewer-bill.

22. Liz Halloran, "No Cake For You: Saying 'I Don't' To Same-Sex Marriage," *NPR*, December 11, 2013, accessed July 18, 2014, http://www.npr.org/2013/12/10/250098572/ no-cake-for-you-saying-i-dont-to-same-sex-marriage.

23. Elaine Porterfield, "Washington state florist sued again for refusal to service gay wedding," *Reuters*, April 19, 2013, accessed July 18, 2014, http://www.reuters.com/article/2013/04/19/ us-usa-gaymarriage-washington-idUSBRE93I08820130419.

24. Robert Barnes, "Supreme Court declines case of photographer who denied service to gay couple," *Washington Post*, April 7, 2014, accessed July 18, 2014, http://www.washingtonpost.com/politics/supreme-court-wont-review-new-mexico-gay-commitment-ceremony-photo-case/2014/04/07/ f9246cb2-bc3a-11e3-9a05-c739f29ccb08_story.html.

25. Adam Serwer, "Why 'religious freedom' laws are doomed," *MSNBC*, February 28, 2014, accessed July 18, 2014, http://www.msnbc.com/msnbc/ why-religious-freedom-laws-are-doomed.

26. George Neumayr, "Religious Freedom's Drip-by-Drip Death," *The American Spectator*, April 13, 2013, accessed July 30, 2014, http://spectator.org/ articles/55855/religious-freedoms-drip-drip-death.

27. Matt Rocheleau, "Accrediting Agency to Review Gordon College," *Boston Globe*, July 11, 2014, accessed October 9, 2014, http://bostonglobe.com/ metro/2014/07/11/agency-review-whether-college-antigay-stance-policies-violate-accrediting-standards.

28. Cherri Gregg, "Local Civil Rights Groups Withdrawing Support For Proposed Employment Non-Discrimination Act," *CBS Philly*, July 13, 2014, accessed July 18, 2014, http://philadelphia.cbslocal.com/2014/07/13/ local-civil-rights-groups-withdrawing-support-for-proposed-employment-non-discrimination-act.

29. Zeke J. Miller, "Obama to Sign Executive Order on LGBT Discrimination," *Time*, June 16, 2014, accessed July 18, 2014, http://time.com/2882538/ obama-enda-lgbt-discrimination. The order can be viewed at http://www.

whitehouse.gov/the-press-office/2014/07/21/executive-order-further-amend-ments-executive-order-11478-equal-employment.

30. George Barna, *Futurecast: What Today's Trends Mean for Tomorrow's World* (Carol Stream, IL: BarnaBooks, 2011), 125.

31. John S. Dickerson, *The Great Evangelical Recession: Six Factors That Will Crash the American Church . . . and How to Prepare* (Grand Rapids: Baker, 2013), 21–35.

32. Jennifer Kabbany, "Judge Awards Embattled Christian, Conservative Prof $50K—and a Promotion," *The College Fix*, April 9, 2014, accessed July 18, 2014, http://www.thecollegefix.com/post/16991.

33. Todd Starnes, "Air Force Academy removes Bible verse from ca-det's whiteboard," *Fox News*, March 11, 2014, accessed July 18, 2014, http://www.foxnews.com/opinion/2014/03/11/air-force-academy-removes-bible-verse-from-cadet-whiteboard.

34. Todd Starnes, "Why does Air Force Academy encourage athe-ism, prosecute Christianity?" *Fox News*, March 24, 2014, accessed July 18, 2014, http://www.foxnews.com/opinion/2014/03/21/why-does-air-force-academy-encourage-atheism-prosecute-christianity.

35. Todd Starnes, "Bible controversy hits Air Force base," *Fox News*, March 17, 2014, accessed July 18, 2014, http://www.foxnews.com/opinion/2014/03/15/bible-controversy-hits-air-force-base.

36. Todd Starnes, "Air Force removes Bible from POW-MIA display," *Fox News*, March 31, 2014, accessed July 18, 2014, http://www.foxnews.com/opinion/2014/03/31/air-force-removes-bible-from-pow-mia-display.

37. David Limbaugh, *Persecution: How Liberals Are Waging War Against Christianity* (New York: HarperCollins, 2004), 45.

38. Starnes, *God Less America*, 126.

39. Ibid., 128.

40. Ibid., 188.

41. Ibid., 140.

42. Ibid., 55.

43. For hundreds more stories, refer to Todd Starnes's *Dispatches from Bitter America: A Gun Toting, Chicken Eating Son of a Baptist's Culture War Stories* (Nashville: B&H Books, 2012) and *God Less America: Real Stories from the Front Lines of the Attack on Traditional Values*.

Chapter 2: Crossing the Rubicon

1. History books are replete with renditions of Caesar's story. For a short synopsis, refer to "Julius Caesar Crosses the Rubicon, 49 BC," *EyeWitness to History*, 2002, accessed July 21, 2014, http://www.eyewitnesstohistory.com/caesar.htm.

2. Herbert C. Titus, *God, Man and Law: The Biblical Principles* (Oak Brook, IL: Institute in Basic Life Principles, 1994), 56.

3. Ibid., 47.

4. David Gibbs III, "Afterword," in *One Nation Under God: Ten Things Every Christian Should Know About the Founding of America* (Mason, OH: Christian Law Association, 2006), 8.

5. Titus, *God, Man and Law*. See note 5, page 4.

6. Ibid., 53.

7. Ifte Choudhury, "Culture Definition," *A&M University* faculty website, accessed July 21, 2014, http://www.tamu.edu/faculty/choudhury/culture.html.

8. Robert Bork, *Slouching Toward Gomorrah: Modern Liberalism and American Decline* (New York: Harper, 1996), Kindle edition location 83.

9. Titus, *God, Man and Law*, 2.

10. So. Pacific Co. v. Jensen, 244 U.S. 205 (1917), cited in Ibid., 56.

11. Ibid. Titus observes:

[These new legal scholars] believed that the science of law contained doctrines and principles that had been developed by a slow process of growth. These doctrines and principles had not been immutably cast at the beginning of the history of man [by the Creator, as Blackstone and the founders had acknowledged]. In like manner, Charles Darwin believed that the species of life, the subject of the science of biology, had evolved over the centuries by a slow process of growth through variation and natural selection. He rejected any notion that all living species were created specially and separately at some definite point in time.

12. Ibid., 3.

13. Ibid.

14. Ibid., 4.

15. Gibbs, "Afterword," 14.

16. D. A. Carson, "Maintaining Scientific and Christian Truths in a Postmodern World" (paper presented at the Christians in Science Conference, 2001), 2, accessed July 14, 2014, https://www.scienceandchristianbelief.org/articles/carson.pdf.

17. David Barton, *Original Intent: The Courts, the Constitution, and Religion* (Aledo, TX: Wallbuilders Press, 2011), chapter 1, Kindle location 405. "Religion and the Courts" provides an excellent survey of the original intent of the First Amendment and its contemporary reinterpretation by today's courts.

18. Gibbs, "Afterword," 16.

19. Ibid., 17.

20. Engel v. Vitale, 370 U.S. 421 (1962).

21. Roe v. Wade, 41 U.S. 133 (1973).

22. Stone v. Graham, 449 U.S. 39 (1980).

23. Planned Parenthood v. Casey, 112 S. Ct. 2791 (1992).

24. Gibbs, "Afterword," 22.

25. Romer v. Evans, 116 S. Ct. 1620 (1996).

26. Lawrence v. Texas, 123 S. Ct. 2472 (2003).

27. Gibbs, "Afterword," 24.

28. United States v. Windsor, 570 U.S. (2013).

29. Quoted by Robert Barnes in "Scalia finds his predictions on same-sex marriage ruling being borne out," *Washington Post*, December 29, 2013, accessed July 21, 2014, http://www.washingtonpost.com/politics/scalia-finds-his-predictions-on-same-sex-marriage-ruling-being-borne-out/2013/12/29/d2c7b90a-7097-11e3-8def-a33011492df2_story.html.

30. Justin McCarthy, "Same Sex Marriage Support Reaches New High at 55%: Nearly 8 in 10 young adults favor gay marriage," *Gallup Politics*, May 21, 2014, accessed July 21, 2014, http://www.gallup.com/poll/169640/sex-marriage-support-reaches-new-high.aspx.

31. "Same-Sex Marriage, Gay Rights," *Polling Report*, accessed July 21, 2014, http://www.pollingreport.com/civil.htm.

32. Ibid.

33. Warren Richey, "Poll finds broad, rapid shift among Americans toward gay marriage," *The Christian Science Monitor*, March 27, 2014, accessed July 21, 2014, http://www.csmonitor.com/USA/Politics/2014/0327/Poll-finds-broad-rapid-shift-among-Americans-toward-gay-marriage.

34. Ibid.

35. Ed O'Keefe, "Republicans warm to gay marriage," *Washington Post* in *Chicago Tribune*, April 28, 2014.

36. Ibid.

37. Jocelyn Kiley, "Most Young Republicans Favor Same-Sex Marriage," *Pew Research Center*, March 10, 2014, accessed July 21, 2014, http://www.pewresearch.org/fact-tank/2014/03/10/61-of-young-republicans-favor-same-sex-marriage.

38. When California passed the School Success and Opportunity Act (AB1266), it was the first state to allow transgendered students to choose their restroom. Other states, such as Utah, have chosen not to allow a transgendered student this right. The battle will rage for the next few years.

39. Os Guinness, *Renaissance: The Power of the Gospel However Dark the Time* (Downers Grove, IL: InterVarsity Press, 2014), 19.

Chapter 3: Normal not Strange

1. D. A. Carson, *The Farewell Discourse and Final Prayer of Jesus: An Exposition of John 14–17* (Grand Rapids: Baker, 1980), 118.

2. Grant R. Osborne, *Matthew* (Grand Rapids: Zondervan, 2010), 637.

3. Ibid.

4. Glenn Penner, *In the Shadow of the Cross: A Biblical Theology of Persecution and Discipleship* (Bartlesville, OK: Living Sacrifice Books, 2004), 137.

5. Osborne, *Matthew*, 637.

Chapter 4: Blessed not Cursed

1. D. Edmond Hiebert, *The Epistle of James: Tests of a Living Faith* (Chicago: Moody Press, 1979), 73.

2. Dan G. McCartney, *James* (Grand Rapids: Baker, 2009), 85.

3. Hiebert, *The Epistle of James*, 76.

Chapter 5: Exposed not Protected

1. Wayne A. Grudem, *Politics According to the Bible: A Comprehensive Resource for Understanding Modern Political Issues in Light of Scripture* (Grand Rapids: Zondervan, 2010), 61.

2. Ibid., 81.

3. Douglas J. Moo, *The Epistle to the Romans* (Grand Rapids: Eerdmans, 1996), 802.

4. Leon Morris, *The Epistle to the Romans* (Grand Rapids: Eerdmans, 1988), 464.

5. Grudem, *Politics According to the Bible*, 80.

6. Morris, *The Epistle to the Romans*, 464.

7. Erwin W. Lutzer, *Where Do We Go from Here? Hope and Direction in Our Present Crisis* (Chicago: Moody, 2013), 44.

8. John Fox, "The Tenth Persecution, Under Diocletian, A.D. 303," in *Fox's Book of Martyrs*, accessed July 23, 2014, http://www.biblestudytools.com/history/foxs-book-of-martyrs/the-tenth-persecution-under-diocletian-a-d-303.html.

9. Glenn Penner, *In the Shadow of the Cross: A Biblical Theology of Persecution and Discipleship* (Bartlesville, OK: Living Sacrifice Books, 2004), 129.

10. D. Edmond Hiebert, *Second Timothy* (Chicago: Moody, 1958), 47.

Chapter 6: Compassion not Anger

1. Leon Morris, *The Gospel According to Matthew* (Grand Rapids: Eerdmans, 1992), 130.

2. Morris, *The Epistle to the Romans*, 449.

3. Thomas R. Scheiner, *Romans* (Grand Rapids: Baker, 1998), 667.

4. Glenn Penner, *In the Shadow of the Cross: A Biblical Theology of Persecution and Discipleship* (Bartlesville, OK: Living Sacrifice Books, 2004), 235.

5. Ibid., 237.

6. Charles Dickens, *A Christmas Carol* (London: Chapman & Hall, 1843), chapter 3, accessed August 1, 2014. http://www.literature.org/authors/dickens-charles/christmas-carol/chapter-03.html.

7. Penner, *In the Shadow of the Cross*, 118.

8. Scott Cunningham, *'Through Many Tribulations': The Theology of Persecution in Luke–Acts* (Sheffield, England: Sheffield Academic, 1997), 287–94. Originally a doctoral dissertation, this is one of few academic works available on persecution.

9. Darrell L. Bock, *Acts* (Grand Rapids: Baker, 2007), 272.

10. Ibid.

11. F. F. Bruce, *The Book of Acts (Revised Edition)* (Grand Rapids: Eerdmans, 1988), 127.

12. Bock, *Acts*, 274.

13. Bruce, *The Book of Acts*, 129. Bruce writes, "It was necessary in Jewish court procedure that the accused person should know what the charges against him were, and have an opportunity of replying to them."

14. The speech is worthy of careful analysis and has been parsed by many. I agree with Bock's conclusions and reflect his thoughts here.

15. Bruce, *The Book of Acts*, 152–3.

16. Penner, *In the Shadow of the Cross*, 186.

Chapter 7: Rewarded not Forsaken

1. Erwin W. Lutzer, *Your Eternal Reward: Triumph and Tears at the Judgment Seat of Christ* (Chicago: Moody, 1998), 12.

2. Glenn Penner, *In the Shadow of the Cross: A Biblical Theology of Persecution and Discipleship* (Bartlesville, OK: Living Sacrifice Books, 2004), 227.

3. D. Edmond Hiebert, *Second Timothy* (Chicago: Moody, 1958), 110.

4. I. Howard Marshall, *The Pastoral Epistles* (Edinburgh: T & T Clark, 1999), 806.

5. Penner, *In the Shadow of the Cross*, 224–5.

Chapter 8: God Our Help

1. The text indicates the statue was sixty cubits tall and six cubits wide (Dan. 3:1). With an ancient cubit equaling about eighteen inches, the image was ninety feet tall (including the stand) and nine feet wide. It was probably overlaid with gold.

2. Charles E. Baukal, Jr., "The Fiery Furnace," *Bibliotheca Sacra* 171 (April–June 2014): 160.

3. It's likely the "seven times hotter" command from the king was hyperbole. While the heat from the furnace was explosive—as evidenced in the death of the Babylonian servants assisting in the attempted execution—the point was to heat the furnace to its maximum heat. As Baukal states in "The Fiery Furnace," pages 161–63, this was probably done with the addition of charcoal.

4. Peter H. Davids, *The Epistle of James* (Grand Rapids: Eerdmans, 1982), 72.

5. 1 Peter 3:9; 4:1, 12. See Karen H. Jobes, *1 Peter* (Grand Rapids: Baker, 2005), 191. Also Wayne A. Grudem, *1 Peter* (Downers Grove, IL: InterVarsity, 1999), 136.

6. D. Edmond Hiebert, *First Peter* (Chicago: Moody, 1984), 172.

7. Jobes, *1 Peter*, 195.

8. Ibid. Jobes makes an excellent observation: "One cannot step into the footsteps of Jesus and head off in any other direction but the direction he took, and his footsteps lead to the cross, through the grave, and onward to glory."

9. William L. Lane, *Hebrews 9–13* (Nashville: Thomas Nelson, 1991), 410.

10. Moo, *The Epistle to the Romans*, 523. Moo gives an excellent word study of the verb *sunantilambanatai* in footnote 80.

Chapter 9: An Encouraging Word from the Persecuted Church

1. Samuel E. Naaman, "Persecution of Christian Minorities in Pakistan," 2011, 10.

2. *Compass News*, September 28, 2011.

3. "False accusations of blasphemy against a Christian, the court invites him to 'leave the country,' " *Agensia Fides*, September 15, 2011, accessed June 21, 2014, http://www.fides.org/en/news/29849?idnews=29849&lan=eng.

4. Luiza Oleszczuk, "Christian Accused of Blasphemy in Pakistan Dies in Jail," *Christian Post*, September 20, 2011, accessed July 11, 2014, http://www.christianpost.com/news/christian-accused-of-blasphemy-in-pakistan-dies-in-jail-56005/.

5. "Christian Man Accused of Blasphemy Dies in Pakistan Prison," *Barnabas Aid*, September 21, 2011, accessed June 1, 2014, http://barnabasfund.org/Christian-man-accused-of-blasphemy-dies-in-Pakistan-prison.html.

6. *Compass News*, September 21, 2011.

7. Ibid., September 8, 2011.

8. *Barnabas Aid*, September 19, 2011, http://www.barnabasfund.org.

9. Naaman, 7.

10. Author's translation.

11. Adam Liptak, "Supreme Court Bolsters Gay Marriage With Two Major Rulings," *New York Times*, June 26, 2013, accessed July 11, 2014, http://www.nytimes.com/2013/06/27/us/politics/supreme-court-gay-marriage.html.

12. Jack Healy, "After 5 Months of Sales, Colorado Sees the Downside of a Legal High," *New York Times*, May 31, 2014, accessed July 11, 2014, http://www.nytimes.com/2014/06/01/us/after-5-months-of-sales-colorado-sees-the-downside-of-a-legal-high.html.

13. Hemant Mehta, "How Many Atheists and Agnostics Are Graduating From Harvard . . . ?" *Patheos Atheist Channel*, May 29, 2014, accessed July 11, 2014, http://www.patheos.com/blogs/friendlyatheist/2014/05/29/how-many-atheists-and-agnostics-are-graduating-from-harvard/.

14. "Guttmacher Institute Fails to Acknowledge the Impact of Pro-Life Legislation even as it Reports Big Abortion's Decline, notes Americans United for Life," *Americans United for Life*, January 31, 2014, accessed July 11, 2014,

http://www.aul.org/2014/01/guttmacher-institute-fails-to-acknowledge-the-impact-of-pro-life-legislation-even-as-it-reports-big-abortions-decline-notes-americans-united-for-life/.

15. David Masci and Michael Lipka, "Fighting Over Darwin, State by State," updated February 3, 2014, accessed July 11, 2014, http://www.pewforum.org/2009/02/04/fighting-over-darwin-state-by-state/.

16. Ibid., 1 Naaman, 13.

Chapter 10: The Hope of Revival

1. Harold J. Ockenga, "The Great Revival," *Bibliotheca Sacra* 104 (April–June 1947): 225.

2. Case in point: William G. McLoughlin in his *Revivals, Awakenings and Reforms* (Chicago: University of Chicago Press, 1978) argues for a primarily cultural basis for revival while J. Edwin Orr, who has often been described as the most knowledgeable man in America on revivals, always links revivals to a fresh outpouring of God's Spirit. I adopt Orr's viewpoint.

3. Ockenga, "The Great Revival," 223.

4. J. Edwin Orr, "Revival and Social Change," *Fides Et Historia* (Spring 1974): 1.

5. Ibid., 2–10.

6. J. Edwin Orr, "The Re-study of Revival and Revivalism" (paper published by the School of World Mission, Pasadena, CA, 1981), 6.

7. Ibid., 7.

8. Ibid., 9. Orr also reports that a committee in Congress was grappling with an absence of justice, such as in Tennessee and Kentucky where only one court of justice had been held in five years.

9. Ibid.

10. Keith J. Hardeman, *Seasons of Refreshing: Evangelism and Revivals in America* (Grand Rapids: Baker, 1994), 111.

11. Orr, "Revival and Social Change," 6.

12. Orr, "Re-study of Revival and Revivalism," 23.

13. Orr, "Revival and Social Change," 7. William Miller fixed a date for Christ's return which—of course—didn't occur.

14. Orr, "Re-study of Revival and Revivalism," 26.

15. Wesley Duewel, *Revival Fire* (Grand Rapids: Zondervan, 2010), 131.

16. Ibid.

17. Orr, "Re-study of Revival and Revivalism," 37.

18. Ibid., 42.

19. Ibid., 43.

20. Ibid., 44.

21. Ibid.

22. Ockenga, "The Great Revival," 228–9.

23. Ibid., 225–8.

24. Ibid., 226.

25. Ibid., 227.

26. Ibid., 228.

27. Ibid., 231.

28. Ibid., 233.

29. Harold Ockenga, "The New Reformation," *Bibliotheca Sacra* 105 (Jan–March 1948): 93.

30. Garth M. Rosell, *The Surprising Work of God: Harold John Ockenga, Billy Graham, and the Rebirth of Evangelicalism* (Grand Rapids: Baker, 2008), 111.

31. Ibid., 129.

32. Ibid., 131.

33. Ibid., 133.

34. Ibid., citing Harold J. Ockenga, "The Mid-Century Turning Point," sermon 1448, preached at Mechanics Hall, December 31, 1949, Ockenga papers.

35. Rosell, *The Surprising Work of God*, 144.

36. Ibid., 155, citing Billy Graham, *Just As I Am* (New York: HarperOne, 1997), 321.

37. Os Guinness, *Renaissance* (Downers Grove, IL: InterVarsity Press, 2014), 148.

Afterword

1. Grant R. Osborne, *Matthew* (Grand Rapids: Zondervan, 2010), 397.

2. Dietrich Bonhoeffer, *The Cost of Discipleship* (London: MacMillan, 1963), 242.

ACKNOWLEDGMENTS

Writing a book is always a team sport. This book is no exception, as I benefited greatly from the skill and support of an army of people. I am grateful for:

Cheryl, my bride and friend, who prayed for me during every step of the process. Your constant encouragement kept me plugging along when I grew weary. I love you!

Natalie Nyquist, who invested hundreds of hours in editing and proofing the manuscript. Your ability to turn jumbled words into cogent communication is amazing. Thank you!

Carl Spiess, who did yeoman work as my research assistant. Your careful spadework provided an abundance of information for my writing. This book is richer because of you.

Duane Sherman, Betsey Newenhuyse, and the awesome Moody team, who gave birth to the project and skillfully guided it to completion. Your confidence in me is humbling.

The Board of Trustees, who graciously provided me time away from the office so I could put my thoughts on paper. I deeply appreciate your partnership in ministry and consider it an honor to work alongside you at the school that D. L. Moody founded.

My executive team, who ably steered the ship in my absence. Steve, Junias, Janet, Greg, and Ken—you are the epitome of a high-performance team. Thank you for adding even more duties to your already-full plates.

Finally I am grateful to know our Lord Jesus Christ. May the discipleship forged in persecution allow me to know Him more.

BIBLIOGRAPHY

Barna, George. *Futurecast: What Today's Trends Mean for Tomorrow's World.* Carol Stream, IL: BarnaBooks, 2011.

Barnes, Robert. "Scalia finds his predictions on same-sex marriage ruling being borne out." *Washington Post,* December 29, 2013. Accessed July 21, 2014, http://www.washingtonpost.com/politics/scalia-finds-his-predictions-on-same-sex-marriage-ruling-being-borne-out/2013/12/29/d2c7b90a-7097-11e3-8def-a33011492df2_story.html.

———. "Supreme Court declines case of photographer who denied service to gay couple." *Washington Post,* April 7, 2014. Accessed July 18, 2014. http://www.washingtonpost.com/politics/supreme-court-wont-review-new-mexico-gay-commitment-ceremony-photo-case/2014/04/07/f9246cb2-bc3a-11e3-9a05-c739f29ccb08_story.html.

Barton, David. *Original Intent: The Courts, the Constitution, and Religion.* Aledo, TX: Wallbuilders Press, 2011.

Baukal, Charles E., Jr. "The Fiery Furnace." *Bibliotheca Sacra* 171 (April–June 2014): 148–71.

Black, Thomas, and Jennifer Oldham. "Delta joins Apple in Opposing Arizona Anti-Gay Measure." *Business Week,* February 26, 2014. Accessed July 18, 2014. http://www.businessweek.com/news/2014-02-26/delta-joining-apple-as-opposition-to-anti-gay-law-goes-national.

Bock, Darrell L. *Acts.* Grand Rapids: Baker, 2007.

Boice, James Montgomery. *The Sermon on the Mount.* Grand Rapids: Baker, 1972.

Bonhoeffer, Dietrich. *The Cost of Discipleship.* London: MacMillan, 1963.

Bork, Robert. *Slouching Toward Gomorrah: Modern Liberalism and American Decline*. New York: Harper, 1996.

Bromiley, Geoffrey, ed. *The International Standard Bible Encyclopedia*. Grand Rapids: Eerdmans, 1986.

Bromiley, Geoffrey W. "Persecute; Persecution." In *The International Standard Bible Encyclopedia*, vol. 3, ed. Geoffrey W. Bromiley. Grand Rapids: Eerdmans, 1986.

Brown, Raymond E. *The Gospel According to John (XIII–XI)*. New York: Doubleday, 1970.

Bruce, F. F. *The Book of Acts (Revised Edition)*. Grand Rapids: Eerdmans, 1988.

———. *The Epistle to the Hebrews*. Grand Rapids: Eerdmans, 1964.

———. *The Gospel of John*. Grand Rapids: Eerdmans, 1983.

Carson, D. A. *The Farewell Discourse and Final Prayer of Jesus: An Exposition of John 14–17*. Grand Rapids: Baker, 1980.

———. *The Gospel According to John*. Grand Rapids: Eerdmans, 1991.

———. "Maintaining Scientific and Christian Truths in a Postmodern World." Paper presented at the Christians in Science Conference, 2001. Accessed July 14, 2014. http://www.scienceandchristianbelief.org/articles/carson.pdf.

Choudhury, Ifte. "Culture Definition." *A&M University* faculty website. Accessed July 21, 2014. http://www.tamu.edu/faculty/choudhury/culture.html.

Clinton, Bill. "It's time to overturn DOMA." *Washington Post*, March 7, 2013. Accessed July 18, 2014. http://www.washingtonpost.com/opinions/bill-clinton-its-time-to-overturn-doma/2013/03/07/fc184408-8747-11e2-98a3-b3db-6b9ac586_story.html.

Cunningham, Scott. *'Through Many Tribulations': The Theology of Persecution in Luke–Acts.* Sheffield, England: Sheffield Academic, 1997.

Dardick, Hal. "Alderman to Chick-fil-A: No Deal." *Chicago Tribune,* June 25, 2012. Accessed July 18, 2014. http://articles. chicagotribune.com/2012-07-25/news/ct-met-chicago-chick-fil-a-20120725_1_1st-ward-gay-marriage-ward-alderman.

Davids, Peter H. *The Epistle of James,* Grand Rapids: Eerdmans, 1982.

Defense of Marriage Act 1996. http://thomas.loc.gov/cgibin/ bdquery/z?d104:HR03396:@@@D&summ2=m&.

Dickens, Charles. *A Christmas Carol.* London: Chapman & Hall, 1843. Accessed August 1, 2014. http://www.literature.org /authors/dickens-charles/christmas-carol/chapter-03.html.

Dickerson, John S. *The Great Evangelical Recession: Six Factors That Will Crash the American Church . . . and How to Prepare.* Grand Rapids: Baker, 2013.

Douthat, Ross. "The Terms of Our Surrender." *New York Times,* March 1, 2014. Accessed May 1, 2014. http://www.nytimes. com/2014/03/02/opinion/sunday/the-terms-of-our-surrender.html.

Duewel, Wesley. *Revival Fire.* Grand Rapids: Zondervan, 2010.

Eberstadt, Mary. *How the West Really Lost God: A Theory of Secularization.* West Conshohocken, PA: Templeton Press, 2013.

Erickson, Erick. "You Will Be Made to Care." *RedState,* December 9, 2013. Accessed July 18, 2014. http://www.redstate. com/2013/12/09/you-will-be-made-to-care-3.

Evans, Tony. *One Nation Under God: His Rule Over Your Country.* Chicago: Moody, 2014.

Fee, Gordon D. *Paul's Letter to the Philippians.* Grand Rapids: Eerdmans, 1995.

Florio, Mike. "NFL had begun considering alternatives to Arizona for Super Bowl XLIX." *NBC Sports*, February 27, 2014. Accessed July 18, 2014. http://profootballtalk.nbcsports. com/2014/02/27/nfl-had-begun-considering-alternatives-to-arizona-for-super-bowl-xlix.

Foster, Marcy C. "Theological Debate in a Revival Setting: Hampshire County in a Great Awakening," *Fides Et Historia*, Spring 1974.

Fox, John. "The Tenth Persecution, Under Diocletian, A.D. 303." In *Fox's Book of Martyrs*. Accessed July 23, 2014. http://www. biblestudytools.com/history/foxs-book-of-martyrs /the-tenth-persecution-under-diocletian-a-d-303.html.

France, R.T. *The Gospel of Matthew*. Grand Rapids: Eerdmans, 2007.

Gibbs, David III. "Afterword." In *One Nation Under God: Ten Things Every Christian Should Know About the Founding of America*. Mason, OH: Christian Law Association, 2006.

Graham, Billy. *Just As I Am*. New York: HarperOne, 1997.

———. *Storm Warning: Whether Global Recession, Terrorist Threats, or Devastating Natural Disasters, These Ominous Shadows Must Bring Us Back to the Gospel*. Nashville: Thomas Nelson, 2010.

Green, Emma. "The U.S. Puts 'Moderate' Restrictions on Religious Freedom." *The Atlantic*, January 28, 2014. Accessed July 18, 2014. http://www.theatlantic.com/national /archive/2014/01/the-us-puts-moderate-restrictions-on-religious-freedom/283331.

Gregg, Cherri. "Local Civil Rights Groups Withdrawing Support For Proposed Employment Non-Discrimination Act." *CBS Philly*, July 13, 2014. Accessed July 18, 2014. http:// philadelphia.cbslocal.com/2014/07/13/local-civil-rights-groups- withdrawing-support-for-proposed-employment-non-discrimination-act.

Grudem, Wayne A. *1 Peter.* Downers Grove, IL: IVP Academic, 2009.

―――. *Politics According to the Bible: A Comprehensive Resource for Understanding Modern Political Issues in Light of Scripture.* Grand Rapids: Zondervan, 2010.

Guelich, Robert. *The Sermon on the Mount.* Dallas: Word, 1982.

Guinness, Os. *Renaissance: The Power of the Gospel However Dark the Time.* Downers Grove, IL: InterVarsity, 2014.

Halloran, Liz. "No Cake For You: Saying 'I Don't' To Same-Sex Marriage." *NPR*, December 11, 2013. Accessed July 18, 2014. http://www.npr.org/2013/12/10/250098572 /no-cake-for-you-saying-i-dont-to-same-sex-marriage.

Hardeman, Keith J. *Seasons of Refreshing: Evangelism and Revivals in America.* Grand Rapids: Baker, 1994.

Hiebert, D. Edmund. *The Epistle of James: Tests of a Living Faith.* Chicago: Moody Press, 1979.

―――. *First Peter.* Chicago: Moody, 1984.

―――. *Second Timothy.* Chicago: Moody, 1958.

Hughes, Philip Edgcumbe. *A Commentary on the Epistle to the Hebrews.* Grand Rapids: Eerdmans, 1977.

Hughes, R. Kent. *Philippians: The Fellowship of the Gospel.* Wheaton, IL: Crossway, 2007.

"Inside the Persecution Numbers." *Christianity Today.* March 2014.

Jobes, Karen H. *1 Peter.* Grand Rapids: Baker, 2005.

Johnson, James E. "Charles G. Finney and the Great 'Western' Revivals." *Fides Et Historia*, Spring 1974.

"Julius Caesar Crosses the Rubicon, 49 BC." *EyeWitness to History*, 2002. Accessed July 21, 2014. http://www.eyewitnesstohistory. com/caesar.htm.

Kabbany, Jennifer. "Judge Awards Embattled Christian, Conservative Prof $50K—and a Promotion." *The College Fix*, April 9,

2014. Accessed July 18, 2014. http://www.thecollegefix.com
/post/16991.

Kidd, Thomas S. *The Great Awakening: The Roots of Evangelical
Christianity in Colonial America*. New Haven, CN: Yale
University Press, 2007.

Kiley, Jocelyn. "Most Young Republicans Favor Same-Sex
Marriage." *Pew Research Center*, March 10, 2014. Accessed July 21, 2014. http://www.pewresearch.org/fact-
tank/2014/03/10/61-of-young-republicans-favor-same-sex-
marriage.

Lane, William L. *Hebrews 9–13*, Nashville: Thomas Nelson, 1991.

Library of Congress. "Bill Summary and Status: Defense of Marriage Act." Accessed July 22, 2014. http://thomas.loc.gov
/cgibin/bdquery/z?d104:HR03396:@@@D&summ2=m&.

Lifeway Research. "Lifeway Research: Pastors Believe Religious
Liberty on the Decline in U.S.," February 20, 2014. Accessed
July 22, 2014. http://www.lifewayresearch.com/2014/02/20
/lifeway-research-pastors-believe-religious-liberty-on-
decline-in-u-s.

Lutzer, Erwin W. *Where Do We Go From Here? Hope and Direction
in Our Present Crisis*. Chicago: Moody, 2013.

———. *Your Eternal Reward: Triumph and Tears at the Judgment
Seat of Christ*. Chicago: Moody, 1998.

McCarthy, Justin. "Same Sex Marriage Support Reaches New
High at 55%: Nearly 8 in 10 young adults favor gay marriage." *Gallup Politics*, May 21, 2014. Accessed July 21,
2014. http://www.gallup.com/poll/169640/sex-marriage-
support-reaches-new-high.aspx.

McCartney, Dan G. *James*. Grand Rapids: Baker, 2009.

McLoughlin, William G. *Revivals, Awakenings and Reforms* (Chicago:
University of Chicago, 1978).

Marshall, I. Howard. *The Pastoral Epistles*. Edinburgh: T & T Clark, 1999.

Michaels, J. Ramsey. *1 Peter*. Nashville: Thomas Nelson, 1988.

Miller, Stephen R. *Daniel*. Nashville: B&H Publishers, 1994.

Miller, Zeke J. "Obama to Sign Executive Order on LGBT Discrimination." *Time*, June 16, 2014. Accessed July 18, 2014. http://time.com/2882538/obama-enda-lgbt-discrimination.

Mohler, Albert. "God, the Gospel, and the Gay Challenge—A Response to Matthew Vines." *AlbertMohler.com*, April 22, 2014. Accessed July 18, 2014. http://www.albertmohler. com/2014/04/22/god-the-gospel-and-the-gay-challenge-a-response-to-matthew-vines.

Moo, Douglas J. *The Epistle to the Romans*. Grand Rapids: Eerdmans, 1996.

Morris, Leon. *The Gospel According to John*. Grand Rapids: Eerdmans, 1971.

———. *The Gospel According to Matthew*. Grand Rapids: Eerdmans, 1992.

———. *The Epistle to the Romans*. Grand Rapids: Eerdmans, 1988.

Neumayr, George. "Religious Freedom's Drip-by-Drip Death." *The American Spectator*, April 13, 2013. Accessed July 30, 2014. http://spectator.org/articles/55855/religious-freedoms-drip-drip-death.

O'Brien, Michael. "Clintons Hail DOMA Ruling." *NBC News*, June 26, 2013. Accessed July 18, 2014. http://nbcpolitics. nbcnews.com/_news/2013/06/26/19156331-clintons-hail-doma-ruling.

O'Brien, Peter T. *The Epistle to the Philippians: A Commentary on the Greek Text*. Grand Rapids: Eerdmans, 1991.

O'Keefe, Ed. "Republicans warm to gay marriage." *Washington Post* in *Chicago Tribune*, April 28, 2014.

Obama, Barack. "Executive Order—Further Amendments to Executive Order 11478, Equal Employment Opportunity in the Federal Government, and Executive Order 11246, Equal Employment Opportunity." The White House website. July 21, 2014, accessed August 3, 2014. http://www.whitehouse.gov/the-press-office/2014/07/21/executive-order-further-amendments-executive-order-11478-equal-employment.

Ockenga, Harold J. "The Great Revival." *Bibliotheca Sacra* 104 (April–June 1947): 223–35.

———. "The Mid-Century Turning Point." Sermon 1448, preached at Mechanics Hall, December 31, 1949. From Ockenga papers.

———. "The New Reformation." *Bibliotheca Sacra* 105 (Jan–March 1948): 89–101.

———. "Reformation and Revival." *Bibliotheca Sacra* 104 (July–Sept 1947): 337–58.

Orr, J. Edwin. "The Re-study of Revival and Revivalism." Paper published by the School of World Mission, Pasadena, CA, 1981.

———. "Revival and Social Change." *Fides Et Historia* (Spring 1974): 1.

Osborne, Grant R. *Matthew*. Grand Rapids: Zondervan, 2010.

Penner, Glenn. *In the Shadow of the Cross: A Biblical Theology of Persecution and Discipleship*. Bartlesville, OK: Living Sacrifice Books, 2004.

Pobee, John S. *Persecution and Martyrdom in the Theology of Paul*. Sheffield, England: JSOT Press, 1985.

Polhill, John B. *Acts*. Nashville: B&H Books, 1992.

Porterfield, Elaine. "Washington state florist sued again for refusal to service gay wedding." *Reuters*, April 19, 2013. Accessed July 18, 2014. http://www.reuters.com/article/2013/04/19/us-usa-gaymarriage-washington-idUSBRE93I08820130419.

Richey, Warren. "Poll finds broad, rapid shift among Americans toward gay marriage." *The Christian Science Monitor*, March 27, 2014. Accessed July 21, 2014. http://www.csmonitor. com/USA/Politics/2014/0327/Poll-finds-broad-rapid-shift-among-Americans-toward-gay-marriage.

Rienecker, Fritz. *A Linguistic Key to the Greek New Testament, Vol I.* Edited by Cleon L. Rogers, Jr. Grand Rapids: Zondervan, 1976.

———. *A Linguistic Key to the Greek New Testament, Vol II.* Edited by Cleon L. Rogers, Jr. Grand Rapids: Zondervan, 1980.

Ripken, Nik. *The Insanity of God: A True Story of Faith Resurrected.* Nashville: B&H Books, 2013.

Rosell, Garth M. *The Surprising Work of God: Harold John Ockenga, Billy Graham, and the Rebirth of Evangelicalism.* Grand Rapids: Baker, 2008.

Saletan, William. "Purge the Bigots." *Slate*, April 4, 2014. Accessed July 18, 2014. http://www.slate.com/articles/news_and_ politics/frame_game/2014/04/brendan_eich_quits_mozilla _let_s_purge_all_the_antigay_donors_to_prop_8.html.

"Same-Sex Marriage, Gay Rights," *Polling Report.* Accessed July 21, 2014. http://www.pollingreport.com/civil.htm.

Schoichet, Catherine E., and Halimah Abdullah. "Arizona Gov. Jan Brewer vetoes controversial anti-gay bill, SB 1062." *CNN Politics*, February 26, 2014. Accessed July 18, 2014. http:// www.cnn.com/2014/02/26/politics/arizona-brewer-bill.

Schreiner, Thomas R. *1, 2 Peter, Jude.* Nashville: B&H Books, 2003.

———. *Romans.* Grand Rapids: Baker, 1998.

Selwyn, Edward Gordon. *The First Epistle of St. Peter.* London: Macmillan, 1977.

Serwer, Adam. "Why 'religious freedom' laws are doomed." *MSNBC*, February 28, 2014. Accessed July 18, 2014. http://www.

msnbc.com/msnbc/why-religious-freedom-laws-are-doomed.

Showers, Renald E. *The Most High God: A Commentary on the Book of Daniel.* Bellmawr, NJ: The Friends of Israel Gospel Ministry, 1982.

Silva, Moises. *Philippians.* Chicago: Moody, 1988.

Starnes, Todd. "Air Force Academy removes Bible verse from cadet's whiteboard." *Fox News*, March 11, 2014. Accessed July 18, 2014. http://www.foxnews.com/opinion /2014/03/11/air-force-academy-removes-bible-verse-from-cadet-whiteboard.

———. "Air Force removes Bible from POW-MIA display." *Fox News*, March 31, 2014. Accessed July 18, 2014. http://www.foxnews.com/opinion/2014/03/31/ air-force-removes-bible-from-pow-mia-display.

———. "Bible controversy hits Air Force base." *Fox News*, March 17, 2014. Accessed July 18, 2014. http://www.foxnews.com /opinion/2014/03/15/bible-controversy-hits-air-force-base.

———. "The city of Houston demands pastors turn over sermons," *Fox News*, October 14, 2014. Accessed November 2, 2014. http://www.foxnews.com/opinion/2014/10/14/ city-houston-demands-pastors-turn-over-sermons/.

———. *Dispatches from Bitter America: A Gun Toting, Chicken Eating Son of a Baptist's Culture War Stories.* Nashville: B&H Books, 2012.

———. *God Less America: Real Stories from the Front Lines of the Attack on Traditional Values.* Lake Mary, FL: Charisma House, 2014.

———. "Why does Air Force Academy encourage atheism, prosecute Christianity?" *Fox News*, March 24, 2014. Accessed July 18, 2014. http://www.foxnews.com/opinion/2014/03/21/ why-does-air-force-academy-encourage-atheism-prosecute-christianity.

Stott, John R.W. *The Message of the Sermon on the Mount.* Downers Grove, IL: InterVarsity Press, 1978.

Thomas, Oliver. "Restricting Religion Will Not Unite Us." *USA Today*, March 18, 2014.

Titus, Herbert C. *God, Man and Law: The Biblical Principles.* Oak Brook, IL: Institute in Basic Life Principles, 1994.

Turner, David L. *Matthew.* Grand Rapids: Baker, 2008.

Vines, Matthew. *God and the Gay Christian.* Portland: Convergent Books, 2014.

Wall, Joe L. *Going for the Gold: Reward and Loss at the Judgment of Believers.* Chicago: Moody, 1991.

Wood, Leon. *A Commentary on Daniel.* Grand Rapids: Zondervan, 1973.

More from J. Paul Nyquist

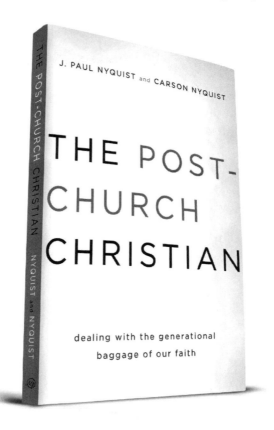

You've heard the stats by now: the Millennial generation is leaving the church.

In an attempt to exemplify the story of Millennials and seek answers for the future, Paul Nyquist, president of Moody Bible Institute, has teamed up with his son Carson Nyquist to share an honest and thoughtful conversation on this topic. As father and son, they've experienced this generational disconnect—both personally and in the church.

MOODY
Publishers™

From the Word to Life

MOODY Radio™

From the Word **to Life**

Moody Radio produces and delivers compelling programs filled with biblical insights and creative expressions of faith that help you take the next step in your relationship with Christ.

You can hear Moody Radio on 36 stations and more than 1,500 radio outlets across the U.S. and Canada. Or listen on your smartphone with the Moody Radio app!

* * *

Hear Dr. Nyquist on *Moody Presents*

Moody Presents is a weekly 26-minute teaching program hosted by Jon Gauger and featuring the teaching of Moody Bible Institute President Dr. Paul Nyquist. This Sunday program also regularly features music by the four student ensembles of Moody Bible Institute, along with student and alumni testimonies.

www.moodyradio.org